Beetle

Animal
Series editor: Jonathan Burt

Already published

Albatross Graham Barwell · *Ant* Charlotte Sleigh · *Ape* John Sorenson · *Badger* Daniel Heath Justice
Bear Robert E. Bieder · *Bee* Claire Preston · *Beetle* Adam Dodd · *Beaver* Rachel Poliquin
Bison Desmond Morris · *Camel* Robert Irwin · *Cat* Katharine M. Rogers · *Chicken* Annie Potts
Cockroach Marion Copeland · *Cow* Hannah Velten · *Crocodile* Dan Wylie · *Crow* Boria Sax
Deer John Fletcher · *Dog* Susan McHugh · *Dolphin* Alan Rauch · *Donkey* Jill Bough
Duck Victoria de Rijke · *Eagle* Janine Rogers · *Eel* Richard Schweid · *Elephant* Dan Wylie
Falcon Helen Macdonald · *Flamingo* Caitlin R. Kight · *Fly* Steven Connor · *Fox* Martin Wallen
Frog Charlotte Sleigh · *Giraffe* Edgar Williams · *Goat* Joy Hinson · *Gorilla* Ted Gott and Kathryn Weir
Guinea Pig Dorothy Yamamoto · *Hare* Simon Carnell · *Hedgehog* Hugh Warwick · *Horse* Elaine Walker
Hyena Mikita Brottman · *Kangaroo* John Simons · *Leech* Robert G. W. Kirk and Neil Pemberton
Leopard Desmond Morris · *Lion* Deirdre Jackson · *Lobster* Richard J. King · *Monkey* Desmond Morris
Moose Kevin Jackson · *Mosquito* Richard Jones · *Moth* Matthew Gandy · *Mouse* Georgie Carroll
Octopus Richard Schweid · *Ostrich* Edgar Williams · *Otter* Daniel Allen · *Owl* Desmond Morris
Oyster Rebecca Stott · *Parrot* Paul Carter · *Peacock* Christine E. Jackson · *Penguin* Stephen Martin
Pig Brett Mizelle · *Pigeon* Barbara Allen · *Rabbit* Victoria Dickenson · *Rat* Jonathan Burt
Rhinoceros Kelly Enright · *Salmon* Peter Coates · *Scorpion* Louise M. Pryke · *Seal* Victoria Dickenson
Shark Dean Crawford · *Sheep* Philip Armstrong · *Skunk* Alyce Miller · *Snail* Peter Williams
Snake Drake Stutesman · *Sparrow* Kim Todd · *Spider* Katarzyna and Sergiusz Michalski
Swallow Angela Turner · *Swan* Peter Young · *Tiger* Susie Green · *Tortoise* Peter Young
Trout James Owen · *Vulture* Thom van Dooren · *Walrus* John Miller and Louise Miller
Whale Joe Roman · *Wolf* Garry Marvin

Beetle

Adam Dodd

REAKTION BOOKS

For all the beetles, past, present and future

Published by
REAKTION BOOKS LTD
Unit 32, Waterside
44–48 Wharf Road
London N1 7UX, UK
www.reaktionbooks.co.uk

First published 2016
Copyright © Adam Dodd 2016

Printed and bound in China by 1010 Printing International Ltd

A catalogue record for this book is available from the British Library

ISBN 978 1 78023 488 5

Contents

1 Coming to Terms with Beetles

I have my own views about Nature's methods, though I feel
that it is rather like a beetle giving his opinions upon the
Milky Way.

Sir Arthur Conan Doyle, *The Stark Munro Letters*

In the early 1980s, the entomologists Darryl Gwynne and David
Rentz were conducting some fieldwork near the small town of
Dongara, about 350 km (217 miles) northwest of Perth, Western
Australia. On the side of the road they noticed the usual assortment
of empty bottles and cans, many thrown from the windows of passing vehicles. But they noticed something else, too. Some of the
small, brown beer bottles – known colloquially in Australia as 'stubbies' – were beset by brown, male jewel beetles (*Julodimorpha
bakewelli*). Since the male beetles are known to harbour no fondness
whatsoever for beer, but do exhibit a long-standing affection for
the females of their own species – who are larger, brown and covered
in a dimpled coating not dissimilar to that found on the bases of
stubbies – it was almost immediately apparent to Gwynne that the
beetles were, however unlikely it may seem, attempting to mate
with the beer bottles.

Gwynne and Rentz published their observation in 1983, noting
that a photograph of a male jewel beetle attempting to copulate
with a stubbie had previously been published in 1980 in Athol M.
Douglas's book *Our Dying Fauna: A Personal Perspective on a Changing Environment*, and that they had now found this to be a common
occurrence in the Dongara area. The male beetles of this species
typically fly 1 to 2 m (3 to 6 ft) above the ground, seeking out the
flightless females. Numerous males were observed upon beer bottles

Variability in
beetles, Staatliches
Museum.

7

(the beetles ignored wine bottles) with their genitalia everted and attempting to insert the aedeagus (essentially an insect's penis). The beetles would not move from the bottles unless physically forced to do so, and at least one was seen to display such dedication to the cause that, even upon being attacked by numerous ants, which proceeded to bite at the soft portions of his genitalia, he would not be deterred. A dead male, covered with said ants, was located just a few centimetres from the same bottle.[1] Anyone who has attempted a picnic on the grass where ants are active will know how quickly and efficiently they can converge on a food source. This predicament did not look good for the beetles at all.

Despite the humorous novelty of this observation, it was an unsettling sign of a larger, more serious problem. The stubbies were not just cluttering the landscape – they were acting as 'supernormal releasers'. The male beetles, 'programmed' to follow up on particular kinds of visual stimuli which have not substantially changed in millions of years, have no way of knowing that a new, strangely familiar yet synthetic object has entered their world. Even more problematic, they are compelled to act on their instinct even in the face of perpetual dissatisfaction, genital mutilation and death. This discovery ultimately led to a redesign of the beer bottles in question, once it was recognized that the beetle's reproductive success might be at stake. In 2011, 30 years after their initial observation, Gwynne and Rentz were awarded the Ig Nobel Prize for Biology – Harvard University's recognition of 'improbable research' and discoveries which 'make us laugh, then think'.

This brief episode in the long history of insect–human relations illustrates how intimately we are involved with beetles, yet how vastly we seem set apart from them. Like all insects, beetles are living curiosities, appearing to us as extraordinary containers of opposites and contradictions, while maintaining a relative indifference to human beings and our affairs. Beetles seem to provoke

A Nuttall's blister beetle (*Lytta nuttalli*) eats the flowers of the milkvetch plant.

our attention and scrutiny with their often colourful and iridescent hues, and their remarkable, sometimes destructive habits. Yet they refuse to give up their mysteries entirely – most beetles, owing to their camouflage, minuscule size and geographic isolation, remain unseen by human eyes. We might not be able to see them all, but we know that a world without beetles would be quite a different world altogether, because this order of insects is a pervasive, permanent and necessary fixture in 'nature' as we know it today. Beetles (like many insects) play a vital role in breaking down dead and decaying organic matter, and many are important pollinators – their everyday labour fertilizes the environment upon which our own existence depends.

Although they may not be at the forefront of our daily, increasingly urban lives, few of us go through life without experiencing at least one beetle encounter, even if we aren't aware that we're in the presence of a beetle per se. This might take the form of an unwanted and ugly confrontation with weevils in the pantry, or something much more enchanting – such as a flurry of fireflies at night. My own childhood in the sugar cane city of Bundaberg, Australia, was regularly marked by beetles as indicators of good things to come. For example, 'Christmas' beetles (*Anoplognathus pallidicollis*), most about 2 to 3 cm (1 in.) in length, would clumsily hover in large numbers towards the lights of our family home during the humid late spring and summer evenings of the festive period, typically arriving after the first heavy rains of the season. Some buzzed brazenly through the open windows, bouncing themselves repeatedly against the irresistible luminescence of the lighting fixtures. Others made it only as far as the fly-screen door, where they joined others clutching desperately to the wire latticework, often remaining there, aimless and 'hung-over', into the sunlit hours of the following morning. And some, of course, ended up on their backs, struggling hopelessly to right themselves.

Perhaps what makes benevolent and benign beetle encounters so endearing is that, for urban, industrialized societies, the diversity of 'nature' seems to be receding from our everyday, tactile lives into the more abstract realms of imagery, memory and extinction. Yet these are realms which intrude into our experience of nature,

A beetle trapped in a purple pitcher plant.

Euchirus
macleayi, Hope
Mountains in Assam.

rather than remaining on the periphery. Indeed, our relationship with nature, including our understanding of what 'nature' actually is, has probably never been more complicated, especially as images of nature bring us closer to it, while simultaneously evoking a distance and often a longing. The sentimentality with which nature is now frequently portrayed speaks to this tension, even while the very lives of many species are at stake.

This is a process from which beetles are not immune. The Wielangta stag beetle (*Lissotes latidens*) of Tasmania, for example, has been included in the Commonwealth list of endangered species since 2002. One of the rarest animals in Australia, it has been recorded less than 40 times, within an area of just 280 sq km (108 square miles), since it was first documented in 1871. Living in leaf litter and moist, decaying wood, it relies on the fallen trees of old-growth forests for survival, and might not travel outside of a 10-m (33-ft) radius in its entire life. The Tasmanian logging industry involves bulldozing and burning the Wielangta forest to clear land for new shoots, essentially destroying the Wielangta stag beetle's entire environment and hence endangering a fragile constituent of the forest's overall long-term health. The Wielangta stag beetle has become somewhat emblematic of controversial Tasmanian land use practices that threaten unique species, but since most of us have no direct contact with old growth forests such controversies seem remote and often intangible. Endangered beetles, in particular, test the limits of feasible and desirable conservation practices. While the extinction of the cuddly, charismatic panda would be a highly visible and very public disappearance, comparatively few of us would notice the permanent departure of an obscure Tasmanian forest-dwelling beetle.

This example reflects a wider state of dissonance between informed concern for ecologically important, localized species on

Northeastern beach tiger beetle (*Cicindela dorsalis dorsalis*).

the one hand, and emotional concern for those species important to increasingly globalized human culture on the other. It is a discord especially pronounced between insects and mammals, oriented by a profound (and perhaps inevitable) anthropocentrism. Yet while we may have largely succeeded in excluding a number of beetle varieties from our increasingly homogenous urban environments, which are to some degree sustained by environmental practices that persistently endanger beetle species, these insects continue to maintain impressive representation around the globe, and have done so for a very long time – beginning more than 200 million years before the appearance of human beings, in fact.

This epic timeframe – 200 million years – is one of many measurements of beetle life that typically confound the human imagination, making it virtually impossible for us to fully appreciate the extent to which beetles are embedded in the ecosystem of Earth. Compared to the beetle, *Homo sapiens* is a very recent and, it seems, highly anomalous animal. Because beetles are among the oldest and most abundant species of animals alive, one might assume that they would also be among the most thoroughly understood. Yet this is not quite the case. There is no single explanation for the preponderance of beetle diversity, for example, although some theories may partly account for specific patterns of that diversity.[2] On one occasion, I was browsing the insect collection at an Australian university. Since I was naturally drawn to the biggest and most colourful beetle specimens, one in particular caught my eye: unlike most of the others, it was on its back within the specimen box. I was surprised to see that its underbelly was iridescent. Since the beetle's underbelly would rarely be exposed prior to death, I wondered what the 'purpose' of this marking could possibly be. I asked the curator: 'Why do these beetles have an iridescent underbelly?' His somewhat ambivalent reply: 'Because they can.'

Beetle, c. 1905–45.

We might not be able to provide a unified account of their variety, but the modern conceptualization of these perplexing animals begins with words. The term 'beetle' has its origins in the Old English word 'bitula', deriving from 'bitan' (to bite), despite the fact that very few beetles actually bite human beings.[3] The English word 'weevil' (a type of beetle) derives from the Germanic term *webila* meaning to move back and forth, or to swarm. More scientifically, beetles are insects classified in the order Coleoptera, a term coined by Aristotle, from the Greek *koleós* (sheath) and *pterá* (wings). Hence, beetles are most readily identified by the hard chitinous forewings (called elytra) that both protect the delicate hindwings beneath and, sometimes, function as rudders during flight. This particular trait has proven immensely successful over the last 230 million years. Of all the known species of life on Earth (including animals, plants, fungi, algae, bacteria, protozoans, viruses and more), about 25 per cent are beetles, with insects (those animals organized into the class Insecta) accounting for about 56 per cent of species in total. This puts beetles among the most abundant creatures on the globe, and were we to characterize a world by its most prolific animal inhabitants, then Earth would clearly comprise a thriving 'insect world'. Indeed, there may be as many

Jewel beetles of the genus *Sternocera*, from Coimbatore in Southern India.

as 300 million insects for every human being currently living, and their combined body mass may outweigh ours by 12:1.

Since the middle of the eighteenth century, when the taxonomic cataloguing of species became an established practice with the Swedish natural historian Carl Linnaeus (1707–1778), about 350,000 beetle species have been identified. Although the study of insects was for some time regarded as a trivial, even childish pursuit, it has been nothing if not productive. The astounding rate at which beetle species have been discovered approaches an average of four newly identified species every single day for the last 250 years. As impressive as this register may seem, few (if any) entomologists believe we are close to accounting for all the varieties of beetles alive in the world today, let alone those remaining undiscovered in fossilized form. As recently as August 2013, for example, 28 new endemic beetle species of the *Mecyclothorax* genus were found living on the island of Tahiti and described by James Liebherr of Cornell University, demonstrating just how many species are still to be discovered. Most beetles (and this applies to insects in general) are essentially 'known unknowns' – creatures we know that we don't know.

Having a penchant for inhabiting niches – various small and specific environments to which they are especially adapted, but which may themselves prove very fragile – many beetle species undoubtedly come and go without ever being seen by human beings at all. Others seem to go extinct, only to make a subsequent and surprising reappearance. The hazel pot beetle of England (*Cryptocephalus coryli*), a once common species which stores its eggs in 'pots' made from its own faeces, was observed to be in sharp decline, and then feared extinct, until a colony was rediscovered in Sherwood Forest in 2008. Similarly, the New Zealand diving beetle, *Rhantus plantaris*, was first described in 1882 from one male specimen in Dunedin, New Zealand. Over the years that followed,

The beetle *Oxythyrea funesta* feeding on a flower.

doubts arose as to whether it was truly part of New Zealand fauna, because it had not been seen again since its initial discovery. However, in 1986 – 104 years later – the beetle was sighted once more, living in a small roadside pond near Christchurch.

Somewhat ironically, the problem of collating all species of Coleoptera into a complete global inventory is compounded further by the sizes of the collections already assembled. While even the most extensive collections are only superficial samples of what exists in nature, they are nevertheless of sufficient magnitude to require searches within themselves, searches which often uncover hitherto unnamed species. For example, in November 2011, a re-examination of the collections of nineteen museums led to the discovery of 84 new beetle species in the *Macratria* genus. The new species span the islands of Indonesia, New Guinea and the Solomon Islands, effectively tripling the number of known *Macratria* beetles in the region.[4] Perhaps even more surprisingly, it has become possible to newly identify long-extinct beetle species even in the absence

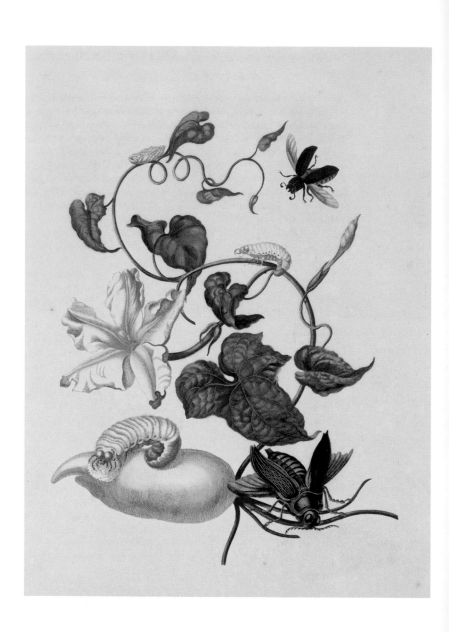

of their fossils. In 1999 Peter Wilf, then an assistant professor of geosciences at the University of Michigan, had been studying eleven fossilized specimens of ginger leaves found in North Dakota and Wyoming. The leaves showed evidence of having been chewed – in a quite particular way. Modern ginger plants are often chewed upon by rolled-leaf hispine beetles, which leave telltale marks behind. Wilf was able to demonstrate that a similar type of beetle indeed had, some 53 million years ago, munched upon the ancient ginger leaf, and he named the species *Cephaloleichnites strongii*. Although these findings have been subsequently questioned (there are other extant beetle species which perhaps account for the chew marks), there may very well be numerous other such forensic traces of hitherto undescribed beetle species for which no direct fossil evidence exists.

The sheer number of beetles means that a 'newly' discovered species, even when sighted directly in the field, may have been discovered previously, only to have been stored in a specimen

Moonflower (*Ipomoea alba*) with *Passalus interruptus* beetle and jewel beetle (*Euchroma gigantea*), by Maria Sibylla Merian, 1719.

Mononychus punctumalbum, or iris weevil.

The whirligig beetle (*Dineutus australis*) is well-known for its ability to manoeuvre in tight circles on the surface of water.

drawer for later cataloguing and subsequently forgotten. There is a sense in which beetles represent the apparent infinitude of the natural world, and they therefore provide an overwhelming amount of data to wade through and sort – a vast body of material that is constantly growing. In many ways, beetles are living embodiments of biodiversity itself. Taken individually, they are animals, or objects, but collectively they are a process of nature. Varying dramatically in reproductive cycle, lifespan, diet, habitat, colouration and form, beetles are as captivating as they are elusive – this is the essential quality of the Coleoptera that weds them to the human imagination, whetting its appetite for a sense of wonder. Variety may be the spice of life, but it is also, just as vitally, the fire of the imagination.

European entomologists of the nineteenth century, for example, appreciated the beetles' diversity as a catalyst for virtuous appreciation and refined engagement with the natural world at large, as James Duncan espoused in 1835:

> The investigation of generic and specific distinctions, which are often so faint and evanescent as almost to elude observation, accustoms the eye to habits of nice discrimination, – the relations which groups and families bear both to each other and to the different kingdoms of nature, lead to general views sufficient to exercise the faculties of the most gifted minds, – while the variety of form and structure which the species present, is the source of inexhaustible gratification to those who delight to trace the footsteps of the Creator in his works.[5]

Although Duncan's prose is considerably more florid than that of contemporary writers, the essence of his observation remains relevant. Studying beetles is not merely something we do *to* beetles, but rather something we do *with* beetles. In this, beetles, like all 'microfauna', invigorate the imagination's attraction to the wonder of scale. Although we may tend to think dismissively of all beetles as 'small' creatures, they exhibit an impressive range of scale within their own domain, varying in size from 0.4 mm (0.02 in.), the length of the ptiliid feather-winged beetles of North America (*Nanosella fungi*), to the 200-mm (8-in.) long-horned beetles of South America (*Titanus giganteus*).[6] The average beetle, however, is around 5 mm (0.2 in.) in length. To put this into a more human perspective, the disparity in size between an average-sized beetle and the largest beetle is proportionate to that of a 6-ft-tall human and one standing 73.2 m (or 240 ft) tall. Moreover, even an average-sized beetle at 5 mm long dwarfs the smallest one at over twelve times its size. Little wonder, then, that Lewis Carroll's *Alice's Adventures in Wonderland* appeared in the popular heyday of nineteenth-century entomology, when affordable microscopes and books about insects acquainted the wider public with the astounding variations of scale present in the natural world surrounding them.

Coleopterists, as specialists within the field of entomology, are more than familiar with the conceptual challenges presented by beetles. They routinely find themselves overwhelmed when faced with the formidable task of making the often fine distinctions between specimens that are required to compile an accurate and thorough taxonomy. Most contemporary coleopterists specialize in just one family or subfamily, perhaps even one restricted to a specific geographic location. Entire entomological careers are based on such focused attention. Beetles are regularly offered by entomologists as examples par excellence of the insect world itself, yet even here the contradictions of the beetle are present. As the renowned coleopterist R. A. Crowson pointed out, beetles are both absolutely typical of and unique among insects, presenting a constant stumbling block to laboratory experiments. This is because there are probably no properties which are common to all beetles but to no other insects, and no single proposition which can be made of all other insects which does not apply to at least some Coleoptera.[7]

Like all animals, the beetle owes its existence, and its continued survival, to a particular combination of chance and resourcefulness. Although some beetle species are unique to very specific locations, such as caves (meaning that the collapse of the cave is probably the end of the species), taken collectively the Coleoptera have demonstrated outstanding adaptation to the ever-changing environment of Earth. Their comparatively small size, in particular, has allowed them to inhabit many niches unavailable to other

Yellow-bellied beetle (*Pachnoda flaviventris*).

potential competitors, and these niches, in turn, have impacted upon beetles' life cycles and diversity of forms.

Understanding beetles in a modern, objective and systematic way requires an appreciation of their astonishing variety, yet this variety seems playfully, almost humorously, to ensure the beetle's evasion of a complete taxonomy. While serious scientific texts inform us that beetles 'may be nocturnal or diurnal, long or short-lived, conspicuous and readily apparent, inconspicuous and camouflaged, retire readily if disturbed or remain hidden within their substrate',[8] in popular culture beetles often come, simply, to illustrate the wonderful, colourful, ever-surprising diversity of nature. So prolific are beetle motifs in everyday design that, like the creatures themselves, we may barely even notice them, yet their omnipresent aesthetic speaks to our deep-seated affection for their kind. Although coleopterists are regularly engaged in the doing of hard, dispassionate science, many of them, it's fair to say, adore beetles, and they are not alone in this fondness. Rivalled perhaps only by butterflies (the order Lepidoptera), beetles are one of the most popular orders of insects, and while much of this popularity has to do with enduringly charismatic beetle species (ladybirds, rhinoceros beetles, scarab beetles and so on), it is the beetle's ability to consistently reveal new forms of itself that perhaps most appeals to the human imagination, across cultures and over time.

The beetle has a rich mythological history, which will be discussed in the following chapter. But what is the beetle's biological story? A classic and oft-repeated anecdote describes how the twentieth-century evolutionary biologist J.B.S. Haldane, when asked what the study of nature could tell us about the preferences of the Creator, replied: 'An inordinate fondness for beetles.' If one holds that nature was created by an Almighty, this conclusion certainly seems unavoidable, based on what we now know about

Christmas beetles (*Anoplognathus parvulus*).

Anoplognathus Leach, 1815

parvulus Waterhouse, 1873

the extent and diversity of the beetle population. But palaeontology has revealed a different, though no less remarkable story.

Today, beetles are triumphantly adapted to both terrestrial and freshwater environments around the globe. Yet it seems to have taken a colossal catastrophe to create the conditions ideally suited for their preponderance. The Permian-Triassic extinction, also known more macabrely as 'the Great Dying', comprised two distinct phases of global extinction, commencing some 251 million years ago. It is by far the most exhaustive period of extinction in Earth's recorded history. It is thought that during this extended 'event' (the cause of which has yet to be identified with certainty), 96 per cent of all species went extinct, suggesting that all organisms currently living on Earth have descended from the surviving 4 per cent. The Permian-Triassic event also represents the only known mass extinction of insects, and beetles were one of the first of their kind to make a lasting comeback. The fossil record shows some specimens of the order Protocoleoptera (as the name suggests, an

Casey's June beetle (*Dinacoma caseyi*).

early form of beetle) from the Lower Permian, 270 million years ago.[9] These specimens represent the pioneering forerunners of the beetles we know today, and indicate that insects were 'beetling' some 20 million years before the Great Dying set in. The oldest known fossils of true Coleoptera, however, date from the Middle Triassic, some 230 million years ago, demonstrating that beetles emerged alongside another notable and prosperous order, the Diptera – more commonly known as the flies.

Despite its well-established earthly heritage, beetle anatomy appears somewhat alien, especially when vertebrate anatomy is used as a point of comparison, or as a benchmark for 'normal'. Like all insects, beetles are invertebrates, meaning that they lack a spine. Metaphorically, this is not good news for them, since we tend to regard spines as synonymous with moral integrity and bravery (crooks and cowards are often referred to as 'spineless'). Beetle bodies are supported by a tough exoskeleton of chitin, a natural polymer. There is a collection of brain-like nerve centres – ganglia – within the head. All beetles have a pair of antennae, perhaps the most emblematic insect attribute, which assist in feeling out the surrounding environment and detecting often vastly remote odorous traces of pheromones and food. Unsurprisingly, the structure of antennae varies dramatically from species to species: some are short and stubby, some are radically extended to a length greater than the beetle's body, while others are composed of delicate branches, resembling ferns.

Beetles have compound eyes, which are often comparatively large, comprising a network of lenses. However, as one would expect, the structure of the eye is dependent upon the beetle's environment: cave-dwelling beetles may have tiny, redundant eyes (or no eyes whatsoever), while others have huge eyes comparable to those of a fly. A few have ocelli – primitive light-sensitive organs, like little eyes – on the tops of their heads. It is tempting, though difficult, to speculate on how the world looks from the point of view of a beetle. The English writer G. K. Chesterton once mused:

> A beetle may or may not be inferior to a man – the matter awaits demonstration; but if he were inferior by ten thousand fathoms, the fact remains that there is probably a beetle view of things of which a man is entirely ignorant. If he wishes to conceive that point of view, he will scarcely reach it by persistently revelling in the fact that he is not a beetle.[10]

We may never know what it is like to be a beetle, but it can be said with some confidence that much of a beetle's visual field is blurred, with objects coming into focus the smaller they are and the closer they are to the beetle's eyes. Some beetles are known to recognize colour, as numerous experiments with coloured insect traps have verified.

The mouths of beetles vary considerably, but tend to consist of mandibles – scissor-like jaws that move horizontally as they chew – and often another set of lower jaws. The mouthparts are often used for catching and killing prey, defence, gnawing into objects for shelter, and sometimes for chewing food. Many predatory beetles, upon immobilizing their prey, vomit acidic digestive fluid onto the victim before lapping up the dissolved remains.

The majority of a beetle's muscles are contained in the thorax, which is joined to the head and divided into three sections, a pair of legs extending from each. The largest part of a beetle's body is typically the abdomen, which is often flexible, containing vital organs, fat reserves and water. Beetles breathe oxygen, but they don't have lungs. Instead, they absorb air through spiracles, openings along their bodies leading to a network of 'pipes' that take air directly to the cells. There is no circulatory system to speak of;

A large male giraffe weevil (*Trachelophorus giraffa*) guards a drilling female.

internal organs are instead bathed in 'haemolymph' – a colourless, yellow or green fluid which moves freely around inside the body during locomotion, assisted by the action of a simple heart. If beetles have a reputation for being 'gooey', it's almost certainly because the haemolymph splatters dramatically when their bodies are squashed.

Beetles have comparatively complex reproductive systems, but in some fundamental ways they are very much like us. Most beetles reproduce sexually. Male beetles have testes in which sperm are produced, seminal vesicles in which sperm are stored, and ejaculatory ducts running through their penises (aedeagi), which transfer sperm to females. Female beetles produce eggs which move from their ovaries through their oviducts to their vaginas, and there await fertilization by a male. Some beetle species reproduce through parthenogenesis, with the female producing offspring from unfertilized eggs, though this is relatively uncommon.

Like many insects, beetles develop through four stages of metamorphosis: egg, larva, pupa and adult. Metamorphosis is one of the most dramatic aspects of insect life to have impacted upon the human imagination, across cultures, for millennia. The wonder

The markings (galleries) of a longicorn beetle, Australia. This species lays its eggs in tree bark and the larvae are typically wood borers.

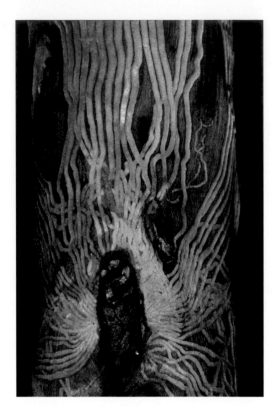

that is metamorphosis is one of the most fascinating events ento-mologists can observe, and although much of what metamorphosis 'is' can be explained by modern science, it is still often regarded as a miraculous event.[11]

Beetle eggs vary widely in size and colour, though most are simple, cream-coloured and round or oval in shape. Some beetles lay a large clutch of eggs, while others, such as the scarabs, may lay just one. The eggs may be placed strategically in a safe place, or freely scattered, depending on whether the mother-to-be will remain present to care for the eggs (most will not). The larvae hatch from the eggs, often during the spring, and many possess chewing mouthparts with which to eat their way into the world, gnawing through the egg skin, known as the chorion.

As is perhaps to be expected, beetle larvae differ dramatically from species to species. Some, such as the larvae of the stag beetle, are chubby, humble grubs. Others, such as those of the diving beetle, are predacious, having a more distinctly insect-like appearance; while still others – such as mealworms, the larvae of tenebrionid beetles – resemble long maggots. In all cases, the major priority for the larvae is to feed, and to feed well. Most beetle species spend the greater part of their lifespan in the larval stage, eating, growing (often very rapidly) and moulting. Some beetle larvae simply increase their size throughout this phase, moulting only two or three times, while others (such as the blister beetle species *Lytta vesicatoria*, or 'Spanish fly') pass through very distinct larval stages known as instars, significantly changing their form at each

Rose chafers (*Cetonia aurata*) feeding on a plum.

juncture. The duration of the complete larval stage is highly dependent upon the environment in which the larvae develop. In transient environments – such as cadavers – the larvae must develop quickly before their food source dries up or runs out. Similarly, larvae developing on fresh leaves tend to pass through this phase quickly too, since their food sources are specifically dependent upon seasonal conditions. Those living in heavy timbers, however, tend to enjoy relatively extended larval stages. For example, the death-watch beetle (*Xestobium rufovillosum*) may spend many years within its wooden abode before pupating. Dry wood, low in nutrients, will typically slow down the larval stage – longicorn beetles (Cerambycidae), for example, may emerge as adults from the timber of houses built decades earlier.[12]

The pupal stage is characterized by a noticeable shift towards the final adult form, occurring during a period of inactivity. Some beetle species in the late larval stage will prepare for pupation by constructing a cell or chamber for themselves in a quiet, safe location, while others undergo pupation in more exposed locales. Most pupae, however, are highly sensitive and the smallest disturbances can have devastating effects on their metamorphosis. The appearance of beetle pupae varies across species, but many begin to closely resemble their final adult form at this point. Some species pupate for extended periods (up to a year) while others get it over and done with in just a few days. When the adult (imago) emerges, it is usually just about ready for the world, though it may be yet to attain its fullest colouration, and its chitinous exoskeleton may not have completely solidified. These finishing touches are typically fulfilled rather quickly, however, allowing the beetle to get on with its adult business. Males and females of a species often differ significantly in appearance, as can members of the same sex within that species. Some beetle species live as adults for just a couple of weeks (such as the Christmas beetles), while others can live up to twelve years.[13] As a general rule, however, the adult stage usually represents the shortest period of a beetle's life.

What the adult lacks in lifespan, it more than makes up for in miscellany. This extends beyond mere morphology, often into the many possibilities of chemical defence, helping to prevent an already short life from being cut shorter still. Perhaps the most notorious example is the bombardier beetle (Carabidae), which delivers a highly pulsed spray of boiling, corrosive fluid from its abdomen, accompanied by a distinct popping sound, when threatened. A whirligig beetle, the water-dwelling *Dineutus hornii*, secretes a creamy, pungent goo when snapped up by a fish such as the largemouth black bass; the fish responds by taking in more water to wash the taste from its mouth, spitting the beetle out and then sucking it back in for another try. If the beetle can make its gooey emissions last long enough, the bass will eventually tire of washing its mouth out, allowing the beetle to escape. Prior to the relatively recent discovery of this phenomenon, bad-taste defence mechanisms in water insects were largely unknown.[14]

While one beetle's chemicals are repulsive to a fish, another's may prove vital to a bird. In 2004, circumstantial evidence was offered suggesting that beetles in the little-studied genus *Choresine* may be eaten by New Guinea birds in the genera *Pitohui* and *Ifrita* in order to 'stock up' on steroids known as batrachotoxins, the compounds found in some of the poisonous frogs of the Americas. Since the birds are unlikely to produce the (very rare) poison themselves, it probably comes from an outside source. Additionally, since beetles are not known to synthesize steroids, the *Choresines* may be acquiring the toxins from plants or bacteria.[15] In a more intimate example of chemical deterrence, male rove beetles (*Aleochara curtula*) inject odorous chemicals into the females they mate with, leaving the females unattractive to rival males and free from possible 'sexual harassment' or interference once their eggs have been fertilized.[16]

Despite the beetles' vital place in the Earth's ecosystem, and the epic, complex dramas that characterize their lives, their success is largely a result of their ability to remain, for the most part, out of sight. Beetles typically like to stay on the down-low, behind the scenes, in the 'undergrowth', as David Attenborough termed the insect world in a BBC documentary series. Many are highly camouflaged, resembling the plants (living or dead) upon which they spend much of their time. There is a sense in which the sub-visible and often invisible domain of the insect world represents a spatial metaphor for the unconscious mind – it is there, with us, wherever we go, orienting our daily lives in ways of which we are barely aware. The intrusion of the beetle into our everyday, conscious reality – particularly the unwanted beetle – thus represents a kind of 'return of the repressed', to evoke an admittedly tired Freudian idiom. Carl Jung famously experienced the beetle's role in mediating states of consciousness, quite by 'coincidence'. In a widely cited

The small hive beetle (*Aethina tumida*), which are native to South Africa. The larvae tunnel through the honeycombs, eating honey and pollen, destroying bee brood and ultimately ruining the combs.

anecdote, he recalls how a female patient under his care was proving to be 'psychologically inaccessible' because she had developed, in Jung's words, a 'highly polished Cartesian rationalism with an impeccably "geometrical" idea of reality'. In other words, she needed to 'loosen up' and accept that the activity of her unconscious mind was a contributing factor in her problematic emotional life. The woman was describing to Jung a dream in which someone had presented her with a golden scarab brooch. Jung writes:

> While she was telling me this dream, I heard something behind me gently tapping on the window. I turned round and saw that it was a fairly large flying insect that was knocking against the window-pane in the obvious effort to get into the dark room. This seemed to me very strange. I opened the window immediately and caught the insect in the air as it flew in. It was a scarabaeid beetle, or common rose-chafer (*Cetonia aurata*), whose gold-green colour most nearly resembles that of a golden scarab. I handed the beetle to my patient with the words, 'Here is your scarab'. This experience punctured the desired hole in her rationalism and broke the ice of her intellectual resistance. The treatment could now continue with satisfying results.[17]

Dr Jung's account, of course, is intended not merely to describe a transcendental psychotherapeutic moment, but to evoke such a 'puncturing' in the reader's own rationalism, to therapeutic effect. A classic example of what Jung detailed at length as 'synchronicity', it encourages the reader to pause and reflect upon meaningful coincidences, especially those involving insects, rather than hastily banishing them to the realm of confabulation and fancy.

I will confess that I experienced a similar (though perhaps less 'puncturing') encounter with a beetle upon arriving in London

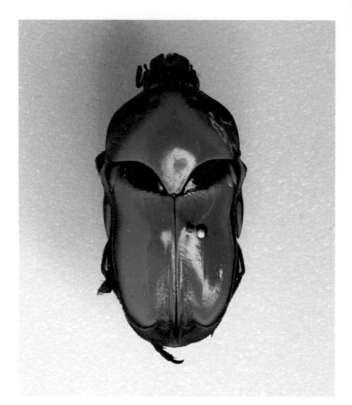

Ischiopsopha bifasciata, a genus widespread in Australia.

American carrion beetles (*Necrophilia americana*).

with the express purpose of finishing the manuscript of the book you are now reading. At the time, I had beetles very much on the brain. Within a few minutes of arriving at my small, one-windowed bedsit, which is not prone to insect visitors of any kind, a yellow ladybird (Coccinellidae) appeared on my knee. Perhaps 'she' had hitched a ride on me from somewhere outside on the busy streets of South Kensington, though even there, I believe, ladybird sightings are rare. Irrespective of how she had arrived, I couldn't help but stop and ponder this unexpected rendezvous. I encouraged the

Stephanorrhina guttata, found in Cameroon and Nigeria.

beetle to climb onto my hand, allowed my vision to sharpen, and watched the little animal scurry about in no particular direction, marvelling as she paused here and there to carefully wipe her antennae clean. Eventually, I released the coleopteran caller out the window. Whatever is happening between the beetle and the human in these kinds of Jungian moments cannot be wholly accounted for by the strictures of biological materialism; the beetle has a vast and fascinating part to play in physical nature, certainly, but this is not the whole picture – the beetle (indeed, the insect) is integral also to the more ethereal, and decidedly less rational, processes of human minds.

When beetles show up literally as 'bugs in the system', however, it is often in the form of a disastrous invasion of crops or food stores, one of the most significant being the Colorado beetle 'invasion' of the 1870s. Others, such as the mountain pine beetle (*Dendroctonus ponderosae*), contribute to the death of extended regions of pine forest, as currently seen in British Columbia. Museums must remain vigilant against museum beetles (*Anthrenus museorum*), whose larvae have a

The Australian longicorn beetle (*Demelius semirugosus*).

38

Demelius Waterhouse, 1874

48759-48761

semirugosus Waterhouse, 18[7...]

particular penchant for feeding on animal fibres and may threaten precious collections. Clearly, beetles can and do cause major problems for the agricultural and cultural lives of human beings, their psychological impacts notwithstanding. But because the overwhelming majority of beetles do not bite, sting, spread disease or seem to interfere directly in modern urban and domestic environments, they are generally regarded as safer, cleaner and cuter than many of their fellow insects, such as flies, mosquitoes and cockroaches. We often spare the most familiar beetles, perhaps even regarding them with wonder and adoration, while other familiar 'bugs' are simply swatted, sprayed or squashed. Broadly speaking, 'the beetle' is not seen as particularly malevolent or malicious, and in cases of brightly coloured or iridescent beetles they seem positively charming, on par with the most exquisite butterflies and moths; to crush these 'living jewels' would often seem paramount to destroying a work of art.

The beetles' relative benignity and aesthetic appeal make them enduring subjects of fascination for adults and children alike. Beetles, for the most part, are tolerable and often charismatic insects, and this means that, from the outset, they qualify for a special relationship with human beings that is enjoyed by few other insects. It is this relationship that I explore in the following pages, a relationship that crosses the conventional boundaries of nature, culture, science and myth. The beetle, after all, has little respect for such distinctions.

2 Sacred Beetle

For the stone shall cry out of the wall, and the beetle out
of the timber shall answer it.
Habakkuk 2:11

Even the briefest perusal of the beetle's appearance in diverse
cultures reveals that this animal has represented many things
to many people. The earliest meanings of the beetle, however,
were largely symbolic and based in mythology. To some extent,
even in modern secular societies beetles retain traces of their
archaic significance. This is perhaps unsurprising, since most
of human history has unfolded in natural environments where
a non-scientific engagement with other animals has been the
norm. Insects have long held associations with the supernatural
and the magical, in no small part because their origins and life
cycles remained mysterious for a very long time. Until at least
the end of the seventeenth century in Europe, for example, many
insects were believed to 'spontaneously generate' from dead and
decaying matter.

Considered as an order, the beetles inhabit a diversity of mythical
roles. Beetles loom large in the history of mythology and religion,
and the case of the scarab beetle (Scarabaeidae) is an especially
salient one in this regard. Significantly, the scarab beetle represents
an instance of parallel mythology – its symbolic expression of
creation, renewal and rebirth appears across disparate cultures
through time, from ancient Egypt to the African Congo, and from
early Christian symbols of Jesus and the Resurrection, to a Chinese
symbol of autogenesis.[1]

Albrecht Dürer, *Adoration of the Magi*, 1504, oil on wood. A stag beetle is depicted in the bottom right.

The case of the scarab's similar reception by diverse cultures makes it tempting to suggest that this particular beetle has 'spoken' a profound, acultural message to us, merely by undergoing the routine stages of its life cycle. Did the idea of life after death predate, and evolve independently from, observations of insect metamorphosis in early human history? Or is the very notion of an immortal soul – essential to many of the world's religions – drawn directly from a symbolic interpretation of witnessed insect life cycles? Charles L. Hogue, founder of the relatively obscure research field known as 'cultural entomology', has claimed that the changes visible in developmental metamorphosis led unrelated cultures to a parallel adoption of winged adult insects as symbols of the soul.[2] While this is an interesting possibility to consider, it may ultimately be, to evoke another animal expression, a case of 'the chicken or the egg'. What can at least be said is that observations of insects 'resurrected' from the apparent death of the cocoon or pupal stage have reinforced various religious convictions that death is merely a preliminary stage to the fulfilment of a more 'perfect' form or state. In this sense (and others), insects do indeed hold an essential place in the history of religion.

Among the many insects to have inspired the production of cultural artefacts, it is the beetles who seem to have exerted the earliest influence. The oldest known sculpture of an insect portrays

Giant scarab beetle sculpture, Egypt, New Kingdom, 18th Dynasty, c. 1550–1070 BC.

Ancient Egyptian dwarf scaraboid, 664–525 BC.

a beetle, thought to be a burying beetle (*Nicrophorus*).[3] The burying beetles (also known as the sexton beetles) are members of the family Silphidae (carrion beetles), and bury the corpses of small mammals as a food source for their larvae. Most are black with red markings on their elytra, and they are notable in that both males and females care for the brood. Fashioned from coal some 25,000 to 30,000 years ago, the burying beetle artefact was designed to be worn as a pendant, probably around the neck.

A beetle-shaped lignite pendant dated from the Upper Palaeolithic period (about 10,000 to 20,000 years ago) also survives.[4] Carved into the shape of a buprestid beetle, it too was almost certainly made to be worn around the neck, possibly as an amulet. Buprestids are metallic-looking, often colourful wood-boring beetles, also known as 'jewel beetles' owing to their shiny, highly attractive appearance. The buprestids are among the most prolific families of beetles, and considering their iridescent hue it is unsurprising that they caught the attention of early humans. The buprestid beetle pendant, found at Arcy-sur-Cure in Burgundy, France, and the burying beetle made of coal, are good physical evidence that Coleoptera held some significance in the very early cultural lives of human beings. While it is difficult to speculate about the precise meanings attached to these artefacts by the cultures and individuals that produced them, the very existence of the objects does suggest that the beetles they represent were seen as embodiments of important powers or values that could be contained, or at least expressed, by reproductions of their form. On a more superficial level, these beetles (especially, perhaps, the buprestids) are simply nice to look at, and the promotion of visual pleasure in the observation of nature is a historically entrenched, and deeply important, cultural practice.

The entomologist Yves Cambefort suggests that one way to understand examples of beetles in ancient cultures is by turning to the findings of contemporary ethnoentomology, a field which examines the cultural place of insects in indigenous cultures. Generally speaking, it is held that for indigenous cultures, beetles have tended to assume importance both as a food source and because of their ability to fly. These are physical aspects that resonate with deeper significances. In many indigenous cultures, shamans are acknowledged as being capable of addressing issues in both the terrestrial and celestial 'worlds' by either ascending or descending into other, less visible domains – much like various species of beetles.[5]

In order to grasp what the beetle meant (and continues to mean) for traditional, indigenous and shamanic cultures, we must first appreciate that, within such cultures, the beetle is seen as a symbolic manifestation of divine or occult principles. Many of these principles relate to shamanic experiences that are systematically excluded from modern Western cultures. As Cambefort notes, a number of shamanic cultures incorporate beetles into their creation myths. In some native South American tribes, a large scarab named Aksak is said to have modelled men and women from clay. In the creation myths of the Sumatran Toba, a large scarab was thought to have brought a ball of matter from the sky in order to form the world itself. In some pre-Aryan cultures of India and Southeast Asia, the primeval maker of the world is a diving beetle.[6] Similarly, a Cherokee myth tells of a water beetle that dived into a watery Lower World, bringing back mud to make the earth, from which the mountains and valleys were formed.[7] The Bushongo of the Democratic Republic of Congo provide a creation account in which, in the beginning, there was only water and darkness. The supreme creator, Bumba, stricken by stomach pain, vomited the world into existence. This took place in stages: first came the sun, the moon and the stars, followed by various animals, and eventually human beings. The animals vomited by Bumba then proceeded to create other animals of their kind: the scarab was the original insect, and hence created

Egyptian amulet of a composite falcon and human dwarf figure surmounted by a scarab beetle, Late Period–Ptolemaic Period, 724–31 BC.

all other insects.[8] According to a myth of the Cochiti Pueblo people, the Milky Way was formed by a pinacate beetle (Eleodes), who was responsible for placing stars in the sky. Because of arrogance and carelessness, the stars were dropped, hence forming the Milky Way. So ashamed was the beetle at what he had done that even today the beetle hides his face in the dirt when approached – here is an insect myth that explains not only insect behaviour, but also the origin of our own galaxy.[9]

The wings of jewel beetles were used to adorn some objects recovered from the tomb of Tutankhamun (fourteenth century BC),

46

while in Japan the seventh-century Tamamushi shrine in the Temple of Horyu-ji was thoroughly covered with buprestid elytra. In a Chinese Taoist text on meditation, 'The Secret of the Golden Flower', the scarab beetle appears as a symbol of the quest to achieve spiritual immortality:

> The scarab rolls his pellet, and life is born in it as an effect of nondispersed work of spiritual concentration. Now, even in manure an embryo can develop and cast his 'terrestrial' skins, why would the dwelling of our celestial heart not be able to generate a body too, if we concentrate our spirit on it?[10]

The scarab or dung beetle (*Scarabaeus sacer*) is undoubtedly the most widely recognized sacred beetle, worshipped most prominently by the ancient Egyptians in a characteristically cryptic manner. The Egyptians did not make the same distinctions between beetles as do modern coleopterists, meaning that dung beetles of numerous genera, including *Kheper*, *Scarabaeus*, *Gymnopleurus*, *Copris* and *Catharsius* (all Scarabaeinae) played important and prominent roles in the mythology of ancient Egypt.[11] For the

Ancient Egyptian scarab with separate wings, from c. 712–342 BC.

47

Egyptians, the dung beetle came to represent the concept of 'becoming', symbolizing *cheper*, meaning 'to become, to come into being; the being, the form', and the god Cheper or Khepri is regarded as one of the many forms taken by the god Ra, who is often portrayed either with a scarab above his head, or with a scarab in place of a human head.[12]

As grand and enchanting as the Egyptian deification of the humble dung beetle may seem, it was based on a fundamental misperception of the insect's life cycle. It was widely believed that dung beetles were exclusively male and reproduced asexually – this established a correspondence with (male) deities who had 'brought themselves into existence'. Additionally, the scarab beetle's habit of forming a sphere from dung and rolling it across the ground before burying it (and himself) was understood as symbolic of the sun's passage across the sky and subsequent 'burial' in the Earth, before being reborn the following day (or in the scarab beetle's case, emerging from the ground fifteen to eighteen weeks later). This had been the standard interpretation of the sacred scarab beetle's place in Egyptian culture, at least since Plutarch's first-century *On the Worship of Isis and Osiris*:

Dwarf scaraboid from ancient Egypt, 1292–1070 BC.

> As for the Beetills, they hold, that throughout all their kinds there is no female, but all the males do blow or cast their seed into a certain globus or round matter in the form of balls, which they drive from them and roll to and fro contrariwise, like as the Sun, when he moveth himself from the West to the East, seemeth to turn about the Heaven clean contrary.[13]

We now know that the male beetle buries the dung ball as a food store in a nest, burrowed either at a location within rolling distance, or directly beneath the dung heap itself. The young hatches from an egg, which is laid into another, pear-shaped ball made by the male or the female, fashioned by the female in an underground chamber of the nest. From here, the larva will then typically emerge from the brood ball as an adult and begin the cycle again. Sadly, the Egyptians seem to have remained completely ignorant of the female scarab beetle and her subterranean labours, believing that the male beetle simply plants his seed in the dung ball, from which his offspring was thought to later emerge. This allowed the Egyptians to associate their view of the dung beetle with the divine power Khepri, the morning sun reborn each day. The beetle was also associated with Atum, to whom the creation of the universe was ascribed, and who was also self-engendered.[14]

Painted plume with sun disc containing winged kheper beetle, Egypt, Late Period, 24th–30th Dynasty, 724–343 BC.

The metallic wood-boring beetle (*Euchroma gigantea*).

Because the dung beetle was so strongly coupled with the concept of its image – known generally as scarabs – became immensely popular in ancient Egypt, and later throughout the Mediterranean region, where they were mass-produced as generic 'lucky charms'. The Romans would wear talismanic rings bearing images of the scarab, and for some time it was believed that scarabs carved from green emerald could improve eyesight; hence it was customary for engravers of precious stones to gaze upon the image of the beetle at regular intervals throughout the day.[15] In Egypt, scarabs were often placed with the dead in burial chambers (often over the heart), usually with an inscription from the *Book of the Dead* on their flat underside. A typical inscription on the heart scarab translates as 'O my heart, rise not up against me as witness,' a plea intended to ensure forgiveness from Osiris, god of the underworld and judge of the dead.[16]

One of the earliest documented reproductions of the scarab beetle is in the form of a small alabaster case, dating from the early first dynasty (around 3,000 BC), which, according to the

British Egyptologist Flinders Petrie, was designed to be attached to a necklace and might have been made to contain a true beetle.[17] Scarab images were also engraved on seals, which were used to establish authenticity and ownership of property. Although some scarabs were fashioned from gold, silver or bronze, and others from many kinds of stone, most were made of talc, which in its natural state is soft and easy to carve. It would then be dipped into a hot liquid glaze, colouring the scarab blue or green and creating a glossy sheen while solidifying it.[18] The trouble with scarabs, as anyone who has attempted to study them quickly discovers, is that there are so many and, with the exception of those made of glazed composition in moulds, no two are alike.[19] In this sense, the scarabs mirror the problem of diversity presented by the beetles themselves. There are nine well-defined phases in the history of scarab making, spanning from the end of the Old Kingdom to the early Eighteenth Dynasty, with each phase producing its own characteristic scarabs.[20]

There are some suggestions, however, that the scarab beetle's influence on ancient cultures of the Mediterranean, Middle East and North Africa extends well beyond the urge to craft seals and amulets in their likeness. In 1975 Hogue observed in passing that the mummy-like pupa probably had been seen to represent the death of the earthbound larva, while the dramatic metamorphosis into a resplendent, flying adult similarly represented a kind of miraculous resurrection.[21] Cambefort followed up this comparison in the 1980s, asserting that, in all probability, the Egyptian mummy is actually an emulation of the scarab pupa, being a temporary condition intended to protect the dead body and the transformations (or *khepru*) it must undergo before resurrection.[22] Furthermore, he observed that a truncated dung heap (from which some adult scarab beetles emerge) resembles a cross-section of a pyramid, meaning that these most powerful of architectural

The dung beetle (*Onthophagus australis*) found in Tasmania and along the eastern and southern coasts of Australia.

achievements should be understood as elaborate models of faecal deposits.[23] It is not clear, however, whether Cambefort's interpretation (which does not seem widely shared among Egyptologists) is based on current knowledge of how the Egyptians actually regarded their own mummification practices, or is a novel perception based on superficial resemblances. In the absence of compelling evidence of the former, the latter seems more likely. There seems to be little evidence that the Egyptians studied or understood the pupal stage of the scarab beetle's metamorphosis. Cambefort observes that 'some indications suggest' Egyptian priests got the idea to examine what happened to the beetle's dung ball when it was buried beneath the ground, and that they 'probably' made the entomological observation of metamorphosis, pre-dating those of the French entomologist and great popularizer of insect life Jean-Henri Fabre by about 5,000 years.[24]

Even so, the idea that the most famous and enduring of Egyptian religious and architectural achievements ultimately owe their inspiration to the beetle cannot be ruled out altogether. Entomologists, both amateur and professional, have often been tempted to draw comparisons between the feats of engineering and construction

performed by insects and those of human beings. Fabre wrote of
the scarab beetle:

> One would never weary of admiring the variety of tools
> wherewith they are supplied, whether for shifting, cutting
> up and shaping the stercoral matter or for excavating deep
> burrows in which they will seclude themselves with their
> booty. This equipment resembles a technical museum where
> every digging-implement is represented. It includes things
> that seem copied from those appertaining to human industry
> and others of so original a type that they might well serve
> us as models for new inventions.[25]

Another, perhaps even more dramatic hypothesis regarding
the scarab beetle's influence on human culture is offered by the
biologist Gerhard Scholtz, who suggests that the scarab's use of
'wheels' (that is, the balls of dung it rolls across the ground) inspired
humans in the Middle East to invent the wheel itself. Given that
domesticated hooved animals were kept in the region at the time,
and that scarabs are attracted to their dung, it is possible that shep-
herds observed the ball-rolling beetles over time and from this
drew inspiration for the wheel. The invention of the wheel was particularly important because it combined the mythological aspect
of round objects with a practical purpose.[26] Furthermore, although
human beings have a long history of turning observations of nature
into technological ends, the wheel is generally regarded as something we came up with on our own, as a 'nature-independent
cultural achievement'.[27] Scholtz's theory presents an intriguing
(but ultimately speculative) argument for the most widely applied
technological accomplishment of human civilization having been
fundamentally inspired by the observation of beetles rolling balls
of livestock faeces across the ground. A more deflating explanation

of the foremost 'nature-independent' invention is, perhaps, difficult to imagine. It also raises the question of why the Egyptians did not manufacture their own wheels, based on their observations of the scarab beetle's efforts – such an invention may have proved somewhat useful in the construction of the pyramids, among other endeavours.

This kind of cultural ambiguity seems to be an essential quality of beetles – while they hover and crawl on the periphery of our cultivated human 'world', they consistently intimate a more profound degree of involvement in our cultural history than we may care to acknowledge. Few of us would readily associate the beetle with historical conceptions of the Virgin Mary, for example. Yet the association is a well-established one, especially in the European folk tradition. In his pioneering work of 1865 on the history of insects in human culture, Frank Cowan outlines the traditional significance of the 'ladybird' (the Coccinellidae family). In Scandinavia, this beetle is dedicated to the Virgin Mary, and is generally known as *Nyckelpiga* ('our Lady's key-maid'), and in

Ladybird of the Coccinellidae family.

Wenceslaus Hollar,
after Francis Cleyn,
*The Fable of the
Eagle and the
Beetle*, 1665, print.

Sweden more particularly as *Jungfru Marias Gullhöna* – the Virgin
Mary's golden hen. In Germany, it has been called *Frauen* or *Marien-
käfer* (lady beetles of the Virgin Mary), and in France is known as
vaches Dieu (cows of the Lord) and *bêtes de la Vierge* (animals of the
Virgin). Its various English names – ladybird, ladybug, ladyfly,
ladycow, ladyclock and ladycouch (a Scottish name) – also reference
this dedication.[28]

The term 'lady-bird' appears in Shakespeare's *Romeo and Juliet* (1597), where it carries the potentially slanderous meaning of 'tart' or 'whore',[29] when exclaimed by Lady Capulet's nurse:

Now by my maidenhead – at twelve year old –
I bade her come. What lamb! What lady-bird!
God forbid! Where's this girl? What Juliet! (1.3)

The description of the *Coccinella* as 'ladies' appears in print at least as early as the English poet Michael Drayton's *The Muses Elizium viii: The Eighth Nimphall* (1630), which relates the efforts of three nymphs to prepare for the marriage of one of their own, Tita, to a fairy, or 'fay'. One of the nymphs, Mertilla, is concerned that they have forgotten Tita's buskins (knee-high cloth or leather boots), to which another, Claia, replies:

We had, for those I'll fit her now,
They shall be of the lady-cow:
The dainty shell upon her backe
Of crimson strew'd with spots of blacke;
Which as she holds a stately pace,
Her leg will wonderfully grace.[30]

Ladybird folklore is especially prominent in Germany, where ornaments in their likeness are used even today to decorate Christmas trees. Here, the beetles themselves are considered a sign of good luck, as they are in a number of other European countries, including England. The German tradition seems to stem from an aphid attack on wine grapes – to which the farmers responded by praying to the Virgin Mary to help save their crops. Soon afterwards, the crops were saved by the small red beetles, which devoured almost all the aphids and thus saved not only the crops, but the grape industry itself. The farmers concluded that their prayers to Mary, also known as 'Our Lady', had been answered, and so in her honour the beetles were named *Merienkäfer* (*Merien* meaning Mary, and *Käfer* meaning beetle), which soon became 'ladybird' or 'ladybug' in the U.S.[31]

Ladybirds thus embody both religious and agricultural concerns – a quality transposed onto a number of other insects throughout history and across cultures (the biblical locust springs to mind). The German dedication to the ladybird as a divine omen was tested in 2009, however, when large numbers of an Asian ladybird species, *Harmonia axyridis*, arrived in Hamburg and other areas of northern Germany. The sudden influx was explained as a result of unusually humid summer days – and perhaps, ultimately, as a sign of global warming. The first European sighting of the Asian ladybird was in Belgium in 2001, and since that time it has proceeded to spread across much of Europe. These immigrants from the east, despite inhabiting the maligned category of 'foreign invasive species',

G. G. Fish, after Anderson, *Lady bug, lady bug, fly away!*, 1872, print.

The Capricorn
beetle casting the
click-beetle's
horoscope, in J. J.
Grandville's early
19th-century
illustration for
Paul de Musset's
*Sufferings of
a Click Beetle*.

Illustration from
Jules Michelet,
The Insect (1883).

actually ensure local aphid levels are kept in check, to the great
benefit of farmers.[32] One can imagine how reverently their appearance would have been regarded in the religious (and entomologically primitive) climate of seventeenth-century Europe.

Perhaps the most familiar folk tradition relating to the ladybird, at least to English readers, is found in a popular nursery rhyme: 'Ladybird, ladybird, fly away home / Your house is on fire, your children will burn!' Dating from the early eighteenth century, this verse, despite its whimsical nature, actually relates to a biological fact: the larvae of the ladybird tend to feed on the lice or aphids

that live on the vines of hop plants, and fire is a traditional means with which to destroy these aphids. When the fire ignites the plants, however, the ladybirds' 'children', too, are thus endangered.[33]

While some beetles may embody the very essence of holy benevolence and grace, others represent quite the opposite. A European rove beetle, *Ocypus olens*, is commonly known as the Devil's coachhorse. A long, black beetle, beneficial to farmers in its consumption of wireworms (the larvae of click beetles), it typically adopts a threatening stance when confronted, raising its tail in the manner of a scorpion and showcasing its mandibles. An Irish folk legend, told in the counties of Wicklow and Waterford, describes this beetle (in Irish, 'daol') as the Devil incarnate:

> The day before Our Lord's betrayal He came to a field where the people were sowing corn. He blessed the work, and as a result the crop grew up miraculously, so that when the Jews searching for Our Lord next day came to the spot they found a field of wheat. They inquired if the Saviour had gone that way, and were told He had passed when the corn was being sowed. 'That is too long ago,' they said, and turned back. Then the Evil One, taking the form of a Darragh Daol, put up his head and said, 'Yesterday, yesterday,' and set His enemies on His track. Wherefore the Dar Daol should be killed whensoever met.[34]

There is, however, only one correct way to kill the Dar Daol – with fire. Any object used to crush it, whether one's thumb, boot, a stone or stick, will afterwards occasion mortal injury to man or animal with only the slightest blow.[35]

In various European countries, and at least since the time of the ancient Greeks, the common dor beetle (*Geotrupes stercorarius*), a dung beetle, has also been associated with the Devil. In *The Peace*, a comedy by the Athenian playwright Aristophanes, staged in 421 BC, the countryman Trygaeus has his slaves feed a dor beetle on the dung of asses until it is large enough for him to ride into the heavens for a conference with Zeus. The Greeks regarded the dor beetle as the 'Devil's steed', and it was similarly regarded in the folklore of central Europe. In Carinthia, in southern Austria, it is known as a *Hexenkäfer*, or witch beetle, and it is believed that if a farmer's wife needs help all she needs to do is keep a dor beetle in her armpit. Three weeks later, a small man – no taller than a human thumb – will hatch, and then do all the work required by the farmer's wife. But he must never be taken into church, because to do so will cause a fire.[36]

Dor beetles have also been traditionally used as weather forecasters and fortune tellers. Various European tales tell of the dor beetle as a familiar of witches, associate it with ghostly apparitions and allege its ability to conjure treasure. One story recounts how, after being driven from a house by exorcism, a particularly vengeful dor beetle responded by suffocating the officiating priest's cow. Yet despite these exuberant associations with the black arts, a French legend tells of a dor beetle that drank the blood of Christ at the foot of the cross at Golgotha – a tale which is almost certainly based on the fact that, when excited, the dor beetle produces a drop of red fluid. They are also known in some parts of Austria as 'our Lord's oxen', on account of the assistance they are thought to have provided to Mary on her return from Egypt, hitching themselves to the front of her wagon.[37]

The idea that at least some beetles reproduce asexually – and thus have a special connection to the purity of the divine – did not expire with the Egyptians. It was retained until at least the end of the sixteenth century in Europe, when the systematic study of insects was in its formative stages. Thomas Moffett's *The Theatre of Insects* is the first book dedicated to insects to have been published in England; a Latin first edition (*Insectorum sive minimorum animalium theatrum*) appeared in 1634, and the English edition in 1658. However, the original manuscript, held at the British Library (and containing many finely coloured illustrations, as opposed to the published editions' crude woodcuts), is dated 1589. The manuscript has a complicated history, and represents a collection and arrangement of work produced by preceding sixteenth-century figures, including Thomas Penny, Conrad Gessner and Edward Wotton, rather than solely original work by Moffett. *The Theatre of Insects* indicates that beetle autogenesis was still held as a matter of fact by some European natural philosophers of the time. Moffett discusses a beetle with a 'Buls horn' – known today as the elephant beetle:

> Like to Beetles it hath no female, but it shapes its own form it self. It produceth its young one from the ground by it self, which Joach Camerarius did elegantly express, when he sent to Pennius [Thomas Penny] the shape of this Insect out of the storehouse of natural things of the Duke of Saxony; with the Verses:

> A Hee begat me not, nor yet did I proceed
> From any Female, but myself I breed.[38]

In an example of the (often complicated) culture of exchange that existed between natural philosophers of the time, the image of the elephant beetle presented by Moffett is derived from a specimen originally sent by Joachim Camerarius to the English physician and student of insects Thomas Penny, who reproduced its likeness. The couplet accompanying the specimen, written by Camerarius, was later reproduced, in Latin, by the Flemish miniaturist Joris Hoefnagel, a friend of Camerarius, to accompany his own illustration, not of an elephant beetle but a stag beetle, which Moffett

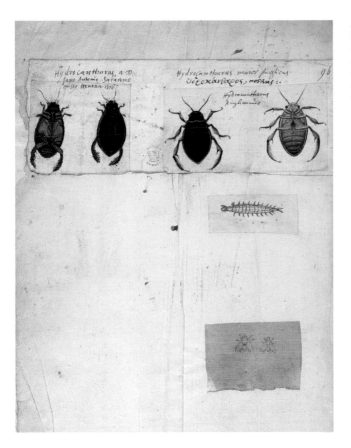

Hydro cantharis beetles in Thomas Moffett's *Insectorum sive minimorum animalium theatrum* (1589).

claims was copied from a depiction in the Duke of Saxony's *Kunstkammer* (cabinet of curiosities).[39] The original manuscript of the *Theatre* contains a pasted-in image of the elephant beetle, drawn by Penny some time prior to 1589, and apparently copied by Hoefnagel and presented in his *Archetypa* of 1592.

The misguided view of the beetle as asexual – in particular, the stag beetle – allowed it to function as an effective, if subtle, referent

Domine ne in furore tuo arguas me:
neque in ira tua corripias me. Quoni
am sagitte tue infixe sunt mihi: et con
firmasti super me manum tuam. Non
est sanitas in carne mea a facie ire tue et

Albrecht Dürer, *Stag Beetle*, 1505, watercolour and gouache.

of Christ. For an observer to infer this symbolic meaning of the stag beetle, they would require (false) knowledge of its reproductive cycle – which would seem to limit the beetle's symbolic meaning to a comparatively small number of natural philosophers. Within the philosophical context of much European natural history illustration around 1600, the fusion of the Antique and Christian traditions led to a distinct, intellectual approach to animals, an approach focused on knowing as well as representing.[40] Natural

Joris Hoefnagel and Georg Bocskay, *Cloth-of-Gold Crocus, Beetle, and Foxglove*, 1561–2.

nterrogauit Jesum unus ex phariseis legis doctor ten
tans eum magister quod est mandatum magnum in le
ge. Magistrum vocat cuius non vult esse discipulus,
simplicissimus interrogator. Et malignissimus insi
diator: de magno mandato interrogat qui nec mini
mum obseruat. Ille enim debet et cætera.

historians were now producing images intended to facilitate knowledge of what the images depicted, rather than as mere adornments to illuminated manuscripts. This new relationship of knowledge and the image was especially suited to the accurate, 'intellectual' portrayal of the smallest of God's creations then known to exist: the insects.

One of the most famous insect images to have been produced within this mode is *Stag Beetle*, a watercolour by the German artist Albrecht Dürer. Finished in 1505, it is usually regarded as pre-empting the kind of reverent attention to insects developed by subsequent artists. Dürer had written that 'it is indeed true that art is omnipresent in nature, and the true artist is he who can bring it out'. Consequently *Stag Beetle* presents a vivid image of the natural subject: poised, purposeful and dignified, it conveys a lifelike countenance and casts a convincing shadow across the canvas, giving the figure a formal depth lacking in contemporary images of insects, most of which appeared in the borders of printed, devotional prose. Dürer had painted the stag beetle (*Lucanus cervus*) at least twice before, however. It appears in an explicitly religious scene, *The Virgin among a Multitude of Animals* (1503), in the bottom left of the frame, facing the centre of the scene, and again in *The Adoration of the Magi* (1504), which portrays the infant Christ receiving gifts from the magi, or 'wise men'; on the step in the bottom right of the frame, an enlarged stag beetle faces away from the scene. In both paintings, the beetle's presence is subtle, but conspicuous nevertheless.

It was Dürer's *Stag Beetle*, in particular, that captivated those interested in representing insects in the final quarter of the sixteenth century, when a revival of interest in Dürer's nature studies was sparked by a copy of *Stag Beetle* in 1574 by Hans Hoffmann.[41] From this period onwards, the image was widely emulated by artists and students of both insects and other assorted 'microfauna'. There is

Joris Hoefnagel and Georg Bocskay, *Scarlet Turk's Cap, Rhinoceros Beetle, and Pomegranate*, 1561–2.

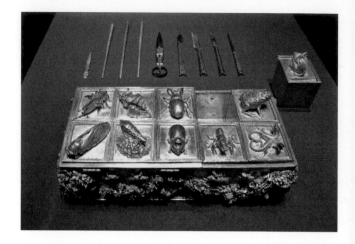

Silver casket with various writing utensils made by Nuremberg goldsmith Wenzel Jamnitzer (1507/8–1585).

good reason to suspect that this image is probably the oldest European picture of a beetle which can be reliably identified to the species.[42] This makes *Stag Beetle* a highly significant intersection of the allegedly distinct arenas of artistic and scientific illustrations of insects, showing that much of what counts as a 'scientific' image has its roots in aesthetics.

Hoefnagel was one of many artists to copy Dürer's beetle, but rather than merely riding on Dürer's coat-tails, he advanced the accurate, 'faithful' illustration of insects in its entirety. Hoefnagel was the first painter to raise insects in their various phenotypes to the status of independent pictorial subjects.[43] Recognizing the power of portraying the singular insect in careful detail, Hoefnagel exemplifies the emergence of what would become modern entomological illustration, but he was still deeply committed to conveying the theological significance of his natural subjects – especially insects. Although all natural subjects were of theological importance (since nature was held to be the most tangible expression of the Creator), this was not simply a case of 'painting

The frontispiece to *Der monatlich herausgegebenen Insecten-Belustigung*, vol. II, by August Johann Rösel von Rosenhof (1749).

DER
INSECTEN=
BELVSTIGVNG
Zweyter Theil.

of beetle = reference to Christ'. The question of the symbolic content of insect depictions must take into account the contemporary belief that each animal, even the smallest, contains the totality of the plan of creation within itself. Since even the tiniest animal is to be seen as an emanation of Creation, they always point beyond themselves towards the whole.[44]

Many of the mottoes that accompany the images in Hoefnagel's *Archetypa studiaque patris Georgii Hoefnagelii* (1592), reflecting on the tragic brevity of life, are drawn from Erasmus's *Adagia* (first published in 1500, but expanded significantly afterwards). Erasmus held that the beetle was 'a symbol of baseless fear, because the insect has a habit of suddenly flying in at nightfall with a horrible buzzing noise'.[45] The stag beetle was taken up by a number of other artists during the seventeenth century, such as the German still-life painters Georg Flegel and Peter Binoit, and the Dutch draughtsman Claes Janszoon Visscher, who copied Hoefnagel's illustrations. It also appears conspicuously in later works, such as August Johann Rösel von Rosenhof's *Insecten-Belustigung* (1746–61).

It is difficult to know at what point the stag beetle 'lost' its Christian connotations, or to what extent the artists intended its image to function in this way. Retrospective interpretations of symbolism in art are often fraught with difficulties; some, for example, have interpreted the stag beetle in Dürer's *The Virgin among a Multitude of Animals* as a symbol of evil.[46] What can be said is that insects retained – and indeed, with the development and application of the microscope, gained – theological significance into the seventeenth century. The pioneering Dutch microscopist Jan Swammerdam, upon dissecting a stag beetle in 1673, wrote to the Royal Society in London that 'Everywhere and in the humblest of creatures the traces of divine wisdom and supreme skill are made known.'[47] With the dawning of what is commonly referred to as the Scientific Revolution, the beetle was poised to take on a new dimension of importance – retaining its emblematic significance, it was also becoming a 'specimen', a Latin term meaning 'something that indicates', itself from *specere*, meaning 'to perceive with the eyes'. With the seventeenth-century appearance of the microscope, and the steady development of standardized natural history illustration and collection practices, the beetle was now subject to a new kind of gaze, which in turn was transforming it into a new kind of animal – an animal of science.

3 Scientific Beetle

The poor *Beetle* that we tread on serves to fill up an order of beings, as useful and proper in the oeconomy of nature, as that of a partridge or a hare, whose preservation and increase we are so solicitous for.

Dru Drury, *Illustrations of Natural History* (1770)[1]

When the eighteenth-century English entomologist Dru Drury referenced Shakespeare, he achieved more than a knowing nod to the Bard. He also exemplified how poetic conceptions of insects retained an association with emerging scientific ideas about nature. These were ideas of nature as a functional, interdependent system, an order that could be observed, verified and described. While it's difficult to isolate a specific starting point for this shift, it is clear that the programme of systematic representation, cataloguing and analysis to which beetles have been subjected began to gain momentum in the late sixteenth century. It was from this period that the beetle was deliberately transformed into a 'specimen'.

Beetles had been described as objects of study in Europe at least as early as Aristotle's *History of Animals*, published around 350 BC, in which numerous species, including the stag beetle and cantharis beetle, are described. Later, the Roman natural philosopher Pliny the Elder noted in Book XI of his *Natural History* (AD 77–9) that in some species of insects, such as beetles, the wings are protected by an outer covering or shell, and that in these species the wing is thinner and more fragile. He observed that they are not provided with a sting, but that one large variety of them boasts very long horns, with two prongs and toothed claws at the point which close together 'at pleasure for a bite'.[2] Pliny also notes that these beetles (he seems to be referring to stag beetles) were worn by children around their necks as amulets, and that Nigidius (*c.* 98–45 BC) had referred to them as 'Lucanian oxen' – a common Roman term for elephants.

Pliny's *Natural History* remained an authoritative and widely cited text into the eighteenth century, particularly its rhetorical passages on the virtues of paying attention to insects. Its relevance and utility declined, however, as disciplines within the natural sciences became fragmented, increasingly specialized, and began to produce an abundance of modern data. Most of the insects discussed by Pliny (with the exception of bees, which had already been historically venerated for quite some time) received his attention because they were associated either with folk medicine or traditions based on superstitions. For example, he notes of the

Jan van Kessel, *Shells, Butterflies, Flowers and Insects on a White Background,* c. 1650s, oil on panel.

beetle that 'there is a small place near Olynthus in Thrace that is fatal to this animal, and is consequently called Beetle-bane',[3] and discusses a number of beetles known to contain the substance *cantharis*, which was also the name commonly given to the beetles themselves. In classical antiquity, *cantharis* had many uses, including being the main ingredient in so-called 'love potions' – the antecedents of the notorious Spanish fly, which is derived not from a fly at all, but from a blister beetle.[4]

The collective, methodical study of insects began in Europe in the final quarter of the sixteenth century. Although insects had of course been observed and recorded prior to this time, it was from this period that the idea of documenting insects 'as they really are' began to orient a systematic, focused campaign. In the late sixteenth century, beetles entered a new economy of natural objects, in which rare and exotic specimens of plants and animals became highly prized commodities of exchange and study. This coincided with an emergent culture of modern natural history, which inspired an intellectual civility at a time when much of Europe was engaged in war over matters of religion and imperial ambition.[5]

Stag beetle carving on fireplace in the John Obadiah Westwood room, Oxford University Museum of Natural History.

Illustration from Jules Michelet, *The Insect* (1883).

The English naturalist and explorer John White was an important figure in the distribution and illustration of natural history specimens in the sixteenth century, producing some of the earliest images of what can rightly be called beetle specimens. As he documented the flora and fauna encountered during his voyages to the Americas, some of White's pictures introduced beetles never before seen in Europe, such as the 'firefly' (Lampyridae), an image which he captioned: 'A flye which in the night semeth a flame of fyer.'

The growing interest in beetle specimens corresponded with a concern for their accurate representation and description, which saw the appearance of beetles in books about insects. Previously, throughout the medieval period, insects had appeared decoratively in the margins of illuminated manuscripts, with relatively little concern for their formal accuracy. Now, images of insects were being produced and offered as aids to learning. The Italian naturalist Ulisse Aldrovandi's *De animalibus insectis libri septem* (1602) is a noteworthy example of this shift, being the first book devoted to

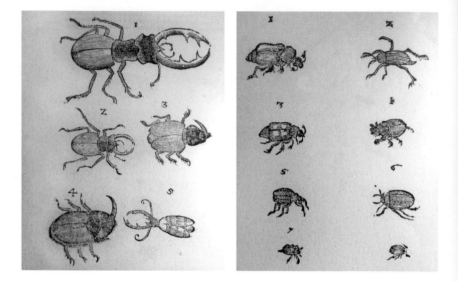

Illustration from Ulisse Aldrovandi's *De animalibus insectis libri septum* (1638).

Illustration from Ulisse Aldrovandi's *De animalibus insectis libri septum* (1638).

the study of insects to have been published in Europe. At this time, Moffett's manuscript for *Insectorum sive minimorum animalium theatrum* (mentioned in the previous chapter), though completed, still languished, unpublished. Aldrovandi's book thus contains some of the earliest published images of beetle specimens, although numerous others had been produced, circulated and reproduced before this time.

Among the many insects described by Aldrovandi, various beetles, including the stag and the rhinoceros, are presented in black ink against the stark white page, examples of what Janice Neri has called 'specimen logic' – images intended as viable substitutes for the objects they represent.[6] But unlike Dürer's stag beetle, these are not especially vivacious pictures. Printed from woodcuts derived from the much finer originals (held in the University of Bologna Library), the images are of admirable formal accuracy, yet they fail to achieve the depth of Dürer's careful rendering, or to match

Hoefnagel's delicate objectifications. In the late sixteenth and early seventeenth centuries, it was not feasible to produce numerous copies of highly detailed, coloured images of insects – this enterprise would have to wait until the eighteenth century. For this reason, accurately coloured and finely rendered images of insects were, along with specimens of their insect counterparts, highly valued by naturalists.

Ring with weevil set in, dated 1794.

Despite technical limitations, it was apparent from quite early in the rise of 'entomology' (a term not appearing in printed English until 1766) that detailed, realistic images of insects were going to be necessary – and perhaps even essential – in the grand project of producing comprehensive knowledge about living insects, their habits and their habitats. On a superficial level, this was (and remains) a case of attracting the reader's eye with engaging pictures of beautiful and surprising objects from nature – an endeavour to which many beetles lend themselves. Additionally, such works were usually sponsored by wealthy patrons who, having their names attached and often being the subjects of the dedicatory prefaces, expected elegant, impressive results. On a more practical level, the inclusion of high-quality images was motivated by the need for the life sciences to develop sophisticated forms of mimetic representation – to essentially 'mirror' natural objects so that the image could, in at least some circumstances, stand in for the absence of the collected object itself, or compensate for the object's deterioration over time.[7]

Beetles, as both aesthetically pleasing and challenging subjects for the artist and natural philosopher alike, were roundly taken up in this project. Trained as an artist in Holland, Johannes Goedaert turned his attention to the life cycles of various insects (primarily butterflies and moths, but some beetles as well) and produced an illustrated volume, *Metamorphosis et historia naturalis insectorum* (1662), the result of two decades of research in the field and raising

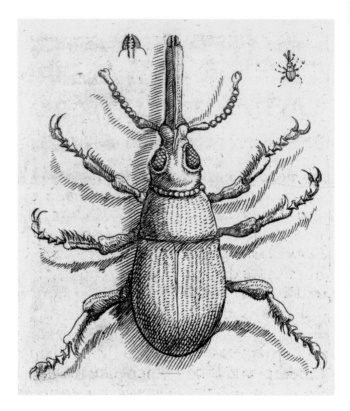

insect larvae under close observation. Translated into English as
Of Insects, Done into English in 1682, it stands as one of the earliest
systematic works detailing the life cycles of beetles. Goedaert
describes the 'Corne Worme' – a beetle larva that feeds on the roots
of corn plants – recounting how, on 22 August 1659, he took
a worm and kept it for one year in a glass bottle with soil in the
bottom, into which he 'injected the seed of *Henbite*, with a *White
Flower*'. The worm, wrote Goedaert, seemed to come from the seed
of those beetles, which eat the leaves of trees and were very frequent

in Holland in May. He found that the worm began to change its form on 3 September, and in May of 1659 the fully formed beetle had appeared.[8]

Despite Goedaert's admirable efforts, however, the methodical observation of insects was still in its infancy, and errors could easily be made. In one case, Goedaert describes some caterpillars he found in a sand hill; the day after he has brought them home, he claims to have observed that 'a Little *Animall* like a *Beetle*, crept forth of the hinder parts of its body', meaning that the caterpillar is 'the Mother of this *Beetle*'.[9] In his notes to the English translation, Martin Lister comments that '*the birth of this* Beetle, *is an odd* Phenomenon' and that he was '*of the Opinion that here is a great mistake, because the like once happened to me: That I thought to have Observed a Beetle borne of a* Catterpillar; *but I question my owne Observation*'. Lister speculated that the beetle had been accidentally brought in, unseen, and placed with the caterpillar – that correlation did not prove causation.[10]

Beetles were still the subjects of a number of myths during the seventeenth century, even while they were entering a period of scientific Enlightenment. Moffett, for example, had included an amusing anecdote in *The Theatre of Insects* intended to affirm the long-standing myth that the oil of the rose flower is lethal to the dung beetle:

I remember one was wont to cleanse privies, when he came into an Apothecaries shop at *Antwerp*, and smelt the spices, he presently fell down in a swound, which one of the standers observing, he went and gathered up some horse dung in the street and put it to his nose, and so a man used to stinking smels [*sic*] was recovered by a stinking smell. Therefore it is no wonder if a Beetle (that we said before was bred and fed with dung) being anointed with the oyl of Roses, be killed thereby.[11]

But while beetle literature of the early and mid-seventeenth century may not have been immune from fable, fancy and falsehood, it was nevertheless able to advance a powerful philosophical revaluation of insect life in general. This was oriented by an impulse (inspired by Pliny) to alter the traditional, anthropocentric view of non-human animals. In its modern context, this move had much to do with the appearance and application of the microscope in the early decades of the seventeenth century. The microscope evoked a new sense of proximity to insects while inspiring a reassessment of the (European) observer's aesthetic priorities and standards. Yet this inclination was gathering momentum in Europe even before the microscope appeared, meaning that microscopic vision enhanced – rather than created – a heightened aesthetic appreciation of insects. Moffett, for example, asked:

> if a horse be beautiful in his kinde, and a dog in his, why should not the Beetle be so in its kinde? Unless we measure the forms of all things by our own, that what is not like us must be held to be ugly. No man of sound minde will find fault with the colour of it, for it sets forth some jewels, and in special the Diamond that is the chiefest jewel. Lastly, no man will think the Beetle at all despicable, who shall consider with himself, that Magicians and Physicians fetch remedies from this creature for the greatest diseases; for they are not only carried in men's purses, but also hang'd about their necks, and offtimes shut up in gold against all children's diseases.[12]

Beetles were not only beautiful (provided one was prepared to appreciate their splendour), but very useful – two fundamental qualities making them worthy of admiration. As Moffett added, in a brief yet profound statement: 'Beetles serve for divers uses, for

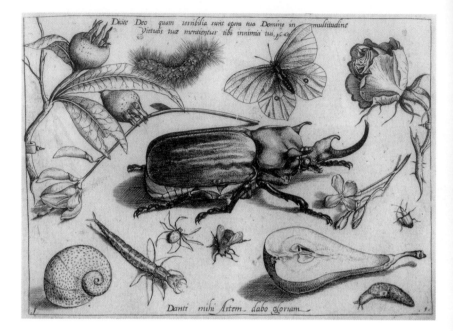

Print by Jacob
Hoefnagel (after
Joris Hoefnagel),
1592.

they both profit our mindes, and they cure some infirmities of our bodies.'[13]

Jan Swammerdam's *Historia insectorum generalis* (1669) is the most exhaustive and meticulous volume on the life cycles and microscopic anatomy of insects to have been produced in the seventeenth century. Translated into English and republished in 1758 as *The Book of Nature; or, the History of Insects*, here Swammerdam outlined his own impressive beetle collection: 'Among these, there are twenty-five exoticks, brought from the East and West Indies, Ægypt, Brasil, France, and other parts.'[14] He also described, in unprecedented detail, the intimate particulars of numerous species, including the stag beetle and the rhinoceros beetle. Swammerdam was especially impressed by the horns of beetles, writing that among 'these insect tribes' nothing was 'more various, or can be more worthy of notice' than the 'beautiful diversity of structure, which is to be met with in the horns of the Beetle kind', adding that he thought 'according to this diversity alone the distinctions of the Beetles into species may be determined'.[15]

Although the idea of categorizing beetles based on the shapes of their horns never caught on, the English apothecary James Petiver agreed with Swammerdam's proposition, writing that 'we shall range this Class according to the shape of their *Antennae*, or Horns'.[16] In the seventeenth century, coleopterology was still finding its feet; Petiver, a formidable but by all accounts eccentric and dishevelled collector with little respect for taxonomic order, also mistook the 'cochineel' insects (true bugs) for the 'coccinella' or ladybirds, referring to the former as 'Lady-Cows', and also to buprestid beetles as 'Burn-Cows'. Of the stag beetle, Swammerdam remarked that the figures of Hoefnagel 'are indeed the best and most accurate of all the figures I have hitherto seen', and that 'when I offered a little honey on the point of a knife to one of these Beetles, it followed me like a dog, and sucked the honey very greedily with its trunk'.[17] Alongside illustrations of the beetles in their entirety, Swammerdam added remarkably detailed micrographs of their inner anatomy, including the 'visculæ pneumaticæ, or breathing, or pulmonary vesicles', and the genitals of the male and female 'Dutch horned beetle'. These images were especially profound, because it had been believed since the time of Aristotle that insects possessed no internal organs.

Swammerdam also wrote at length on the rhinoceros beetle, introducing his chapter 'The very curious history of the Nasicornis, or Rhinoceros, or horned Beetle, illustrated with accurate figures' with an enduring quote from Pliny's *Natural History*, one taken up by numerous natural philosophers of the Renaissance period who were attending to insects and seeking to validate their investigations:

We admire the shoulders of Elephants that carry towers; the necks of Bulls, and the furious tosses from their horns; the ravages of Tigers, and the manes of Lions: but we should know that nature is no where more complete and perfect than in the smallest objects.[18]

Golden tortoise beetle (*Charidotella sexpunctata*).

Pliny's observation, which had been made without the assistance of a microscope, and indeed without a magnifying lens of any kind, spoke to the patient, attentive philosopher's ability to revalue nature's smallest creatures through a combination of focused looking and cognitive empathy. The beetle was an important catalyst for this process. Swammerdam, devoutly religious to the point of obsession and keen (like many of his contemporaries) to advance the pursuit of microscopical knowledge, followed Pliny's example, assuring his readers that 'it be made clearer than the sun at noon, that as many natural mysteries are hidden in the narrow compass of the most vile and contemptible of animals, as in the vast viscera of the largest'.[19]

Larva of the seven-spot ladybird (*Coccinella septempunctata*).

85

Swammerdam seems to have been absolutely under the spell of insects, convinced that the investigation of nature's smallest parts was tantamount to the revelation of the Creator's omnipotence – to know the insect in detail was to know the particulars of God. And this led him to some very outlandish areas indeed; among them, the sex lives of rhinoceros beetles. Swammerdam explained that these beetles are usually found in the docks and yards, among the chips and sawdust, in old trees, rotten wood and the ashes of reeds used in the tarring of ships. He then continued, describing how

> the male gets upon the female, and with the horny or bony part of its penis, as with two crooked claws, fixes himself upon the horny or bony part, which constitutes the vulva of the female; by this means the female cannot escape, and the male in this manner injects his sperm, which it has in great quantity, and so impregnates the female.[20]

This kind of description of the intimate, dramatic, microscopic events of the insect world would become commonplace in many books about insects, reaching their literary zenith in the late nineteenth-century works of Jean-Henri Fabre, before being supplanted by the immediate, descriptive power of microcinematic imagery.

The culture of attentive looking that corresponded with the microscope in the seventeenth century inevitably led to investigations of how insects themselves see the world; again, beetles were of interest here. In May of 1698, the self-made Dutch microscopist Antony van Leeuwenhoek wrote a letter to the Royal Society in London detailing his recent examinations of a beetle's eye through his own single-lens microscopes. 'I have, last Summer', he wrote, 'shewn to several English Gentlemen, the Multiplicity of Eyes that

Bhawani Das,
Black Beetle,
c. 1777–83,
watercolour.

are to be seen in the *Tunica Cornea* of a Beetle, that is called the Eye.'[21] The method for validating microscopic observations that developed in the seventeenth century involved the verification of the observation by 'Gentlemen' – understood as cultured, educated males of high social standing and, it was assumed, credibility. Leeuwenhoek lacked these qualities (being a draper by trade, never having attended university, and illiterate in Latin) and so he often relied on reference to the Gentlemen with whom he surrounded himself in order to lend integrity to his novel observations. 'This sight was very strange to said English Gentlemen', Leeuwenhoek continued, 'because, that if one will reproach a Man with Blindness, or Dimness of Sight, they use to say in English, *You are as Blind as a Beetle*, because they reckon a Beetle to be Blind.'[22] Leeuwenhoek was seemingly mistaking the multiplicity of lenses for a multiplicity of eyes, writing of the 'Multiplicity of Eyes' which he had several times shown to 'Persons of Quality' who could 'clearly discern the shewing of some hundreds of Eyes at once clearly'.[23]

The question of what an insect sees of its environment was partly answered in the nineteenth century by Sigmund Exner's experiments with the eyes of a beetle (*Lampyris spld.*, otherwise known as a glow-worm). In 1891 he published *Die physiologie der facettierten Augen von Krebsen und Insekten* (The Physiology of the Faceted Eyes of Crustaceans and Insects), which includes an image

Beetles in Maria Sibylla Merian, *Insects of Surinam* (1705).

To Richard Lyddill Esq.
This Plate is humbly dedicated by Eleaz. Albin.

Life cycle of a brown beetle, or May beetle, from Eleazar Albin's *A Natural History of English Insects*.

of a church bell tower produced using the beetle's eye as a lens. While such simulations may not ultimately tell us much about a beetle's visual *experience*, they do provide some insight into how the beetle's eye functions mechanically in the presence of light. Insect eyes are now known to be of two basic types, compound (or multifaceted) and simple (or single chambered). Compound eyes are either appositional, in which each receptor cluster has its own lens, or superpositional, in which the image at any point on the retina is the product of many lenses.

As the 'dispassionate', fact-making science of entomology began to take shape in the late seventeenth and early eighteenth centuries, aesthetics – the pleasure of looking and the appreciation of what was being looked at – remained important to the image-making process. Indeed, a new form of aesthetic gratification was enabled by images that convincingly depicted natural objects 'as they really were'. A 'realistic' image was, within the emergent culture of modern natural history, a beautiful image.

An important historical figure in this regard is the German artist and proto-entomologist Maria Sibylla Merian (1647–1717). Merian has become a something of a legendary figure in the study of natural history, primarily owing to her unrivalled pairing of tantalizing aesthetic sensibilities with accurate renderings of insects, their life stages and their host plants. She began to systematically study the metamorphoses of insects in 1674, though she was already rearing and observing silkworms at the age of eleven. In 1679 she published the first part of her debut volume, *Verwandelung und sonderbare Blumen-nahrung* (The Wondrous Transformation of Caterpillars and their Remarkable Diet of Flowers), including 50 coloured quarto plates. The second part followed in 1683. Her early work was concerned with the life stages of butterflies, but later, in *Metamorphosis insectorum surinamensium* (1705), her most famous work, based on her studies abroad in Surinam, beetles made their appearance among the 60 copperplate engravings. Apart from the striking execution of her illustrations, Merian was careful to present insects with their host plants, ensuring entomological and botanical accuracy. The results are beautiful, pioneering images that, even today, can function reliably as learning aids while appealing to enduring aesthetic sensibilities. This was entirely deliberate, too, as Merian wrote in the preface to *Metamorphosis*:

I had the plates engraved by the most renowned masters, and used the best paper in order to please both the connoisseurs of art and the amateur naturalists interested in insects and plants. It will also give me great pleasure to hear that I have achieved my aim at the same time as giving people pleasure.[24]

Merian was aware of insect metamorphosis at a time when many naturalists still held that insects reproduce through spontaneous generation. In the late seventeenth century, she began preparing what became known as her 'book of notes and studies', jotting down notes and adding illustrations as preparation for her more major works. Here, she uses a number of terms to describe the various developmental stages of Coleoptera, including 'seeds', 'worm', 'maggot', 'date kernel' and 'woodworms' – beetle larvae found in wood. As well as helping to establish standards of aesthetics and accuracy for subsequent entomological illustration in general, Merian's *Metamorphosis* inaugurated a new century of illustrated insect books – the eighteenth century would see the burgeoning of large, lavish and colourful volumes dedicated to the careful illustration of domestic and exotic insect specimens. Works of this period came to be judged as much by the refinement of their illustrations as by the accuracy of their catalogues.

There are a few especially notable examples of early eighteenth-century illustrations of insects influenced by the style of Merian. One is found in the German naturalist and miniaturist August Johann Rösel von Rosenhof, who produced a number of finely illustrated works, including the multi-volume serial *Insecten-Belustigung*, or 'Insect Entertainment' (1746–61). In the second volume of this work (1749), Rösel von Rosenhof presents numerous descriptions of beetles and their life cycles. Apart from their detail and accuracy, what makes these images

Hercules beetle (*Dynastes hercules*), from the collection of the Museum of Toulouse.

especially interesting is their intimation of 'scenes' – the beetles and other assorted microfauna are presented not merely as flat, lifeless specimens on a page, or within a cabinet, but in many instances as the inhabitants of a lively, miniature world to which the human observer is now being made privy. Even in those plates which portray beetles against a stark, white background, Rösel resists the overemphasis of geometrical arrangement which would come to dominate entomological illustration in the years that followed. This gives his illustrations an enduring charm – even while they continue to function as entomologically accurate images of important specimens.

Another figure of note is the English watercolour painter and naturalist Eleazar Albin. In *A Natural History of English Insects* (1720), a sumptuous volume containing 100 coloured copper plates, each dedicated to an individual sponsor, Albin presented attractive illustrations of various insects in their life stages – mostly butterflies and moths, but including some beetles as well. For Albin, like so many of his predecessors, insect metamorphosis was to be taken as direct evidence of the divine in nature – he wrote of 'the infinite

H. J. Ruprecht, 'Caterpillar, Beetle and Larva: Three Figures', from *Wand-Atlas für den Unterricht in der Naturgeschichte aller drei Reice*, vol. III (1877), chromolithograph.

92

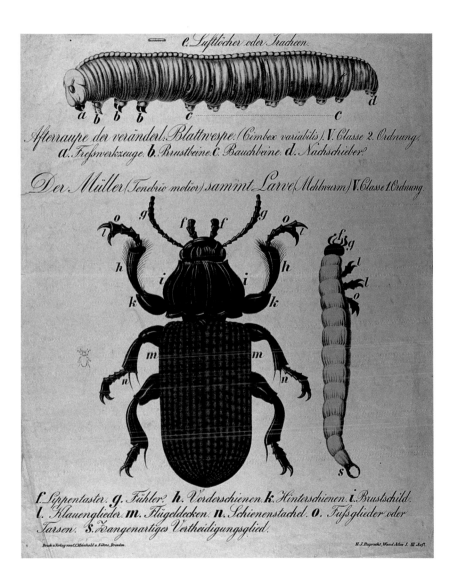

e. Luftlöcher oder Tracheen.

a b b b c .... c d

Afterraupe der veränderl: Blattwespe (Cimbex variabilis). V. Classe 2. Ordnung.
a. *Freßwerkzeuge.* **b.** *Brustbeine.* **c.** *Bauchbeine.* **d.** *Nachschieber.*

Der Müller (Tenebrio molitor) sammt Larve (Mehlwurm) V. Classe 1. Ordnung.

f. *Lippentaster.* **g.** *Fühler.* **h.** *Vorderschienen.* **k.** *Hinterschienen.* **i.** *Brustschild.*
l. *Klauenglieder.* **m.** *Flügeldecken.* **n.** *Schienenstachel.* **o.** *Fußglieder oder*
Tarsen. **s.** *Zangenartiges Vertheidigungsglied.*

Druck u. Verlag von C. C. Meinhold u. Söhne, Dresden.   H. J. Ruprecht, Wand-Atlas I. III. Aufl.

Goodness of God, who in his Providence has given an Instinct to all his animal Creatures, even of the lowest Orders, sufficient to direct them in all Things necessary for their own Preservation, and Propagation of their Kind'.[25]

Albin's description of the sixtieth plate in *A Natural History* provides a customary narrative account of his initial encounter with the insect, his collection of it, and his subsequent observation of its life stages, accompanied by an impressive illustration. He found many of the '*Grubs* or *Worms*' by following a plough, and observed that 'the *Crows* and *Rooks* were very diligent in picking them up'. He then put several of them into a box, 'in which they killed one another with their *Nippers*'. Those that remained were placed in a pot of soil with the roots of grass and other plants. They eventually changed into a chrysalis, and then 'came forth a brown *Beetle* called the *Chafer*, *Oak Web*, or *May Beetle*', both male and female.[26]

It is somewhat amusing to picture a relatively refined English gentleman such as Albin browsing a freshly ploughed field, competing with crows and rooks for the pick of the newly turned-up grubs – especially since a serious interest in insects (and natural objects in general) was not yet a widely respected pursuit, or at least not as widely respected as its practitioners would perhaps have preferred. Even 50 years later, Dru Drury would lament in his *Illustrations of Natural History* (1770) the 'sneer and contempt thrown on it by men of narrow minds, who are impatient at hearing of persons bestowing their time in collecting a plant, an insect, or a stone'.[27]

Such sneer and contempt, however, did little to deter the amassing of extensive collections of natural objects, an enterprise which became increasingly international in scope throughout the eighteenth century. Sir Hans Sloane, whose vast collection of natural objects and antiquities formed the basis for the British Museum and the Natural History Museum in London, returned from a journey to Jamaica with an impressive array of new plant and animal specimens, including some beetles. These he described in *A Voyage to the Islands Madera, Barbados, Nieves, S. Christophers and Jamaica, with the Natural History of the Herbs and Trees, Four-footed Beasts, Fishes, Birds, Insects, Reptiles, &c. Of the last of those Islands*. The first volume appeared in 1707 and the second, somewhat delayed, in 1725. Sloane included illustrations of a number of beetles among the other plants and animal specimens he collected throughout his voyage. Of the 'Fire-Fly' (Lampyridae), he wrote:

They fly about everywhere in the Savannas, and about Woods in the night. The Women work by them, and the Indians travel with them fasten'd to their Feet and Heads . . . in his *Coronica* [Oviedo y Valdés, 1478–1557] says the Indians spin, weave, boil, paint, dance etc by their Light in the Night. They hunt *Hutias* [large local rodents] with them in the Night, and fish; tied to their great Toes and Hands they travel as with Flambeaux and Torches. The Spaniards read letters by them. They kill the Mosquito's which hinder them from Sleep, and for this Reason the Indians carry them to their Houses, more than for Light. They take with them Firebrands, when calling them by their Name, they come to the Light; or with Branches, not being able to rise when knock'd down by them, whosoever anoints his Hands or Face with these, Stars seem to burn, frighting People; a marvellous water, he fancies, would come from them if distill'd.[28]

Perhaps not all of Oviedo's observations, by way of Sloane, should be taken at face value. Sloane admits it is unlikely that the beetles would come because their names are called; it seems more plausible that they are simply attracted to the light of the 'Firebrands'. But

Frontispiece to
C. G. Jablonsky,
*Natursystem aller
bekannten* . . .
(1785–1806).

overall the account does show that beetles were well incorporated into the daily cultural lives of the native inhabitants of Jamaica and the Caribbean in ways that the European explorers found both charming and surprising.

The eighteenth century saw a significant though generally under-acknowledged development that greatly assisted the scientific investigation of beetles – the manufacture of pins. In *The Wealth of Nations* (1776) Adam Smith famously referred to pin-making as an example of the efficiency that could be achieved by the division of labour. In the early eighteenth century, English pin-making was based in London, Bristol and Gloucester, comprising around 100 'manufactories', and by 1735 pin-making had become the chief industry of Gloucester, which was at this time the largest pin-making centre in Great Britain.[29] Pins of various sizes were mostly intended for tailoring garments and fastening documents together, but they had been used by some insect collectors even prior to 1700: 'As early as the 1680s, [William] Courten gave Posthumus Salwey directions that butterflies were to be "fastened with pins to a box".'[30]

However, pins remained expensive until mass-production machinery was developed in the early 1800s, and no pins were made specifically for entomological use before this time. Throughout the eighteenth century, pins were hand-made using factory processes and outsourced labour.[31] Prior to the ready availability of pins, some insect specimens would be kept in jars, which also were not especially cheap or abundant. Alternatively, some were preserved, with varying degrees of success, between the pages of books, much like plant specimens. This method largely limited the collector to butterflies and moths, although some beetles did make it between the pages of the herbaria of seventeenth-century English botanists such as Adam Buddle and Leonard Plukenet. Insects could also be preserved between transparent sheets of

mica, although this method, too, placed restrictions on the insect species which could be kept – the bulbous bodies of many beetles were simply not suitable. James Petiver issued his *Brief Directions for the Easie Making and Preserving Collections of all Natural Curiosities* around 1700, originally in a single folio sheet. Here, he advised that:

In relation to INSECTS, as Beetles, Spiders, Grasshopper, Bees, Wasps, Flies, etc, these may be drowned altogether, as soon as Caught in a little wide Mouth'd Glass, or Vial, half full of Spirits, which you may carry in your Pocket. But all Butterflies or Moths, as have mealy Wings, whose Colours may be rub'd off, with the Fingers these must be put into any small Printed Book, as soon as caught, after the manner you do ye plants.[32]

Although Petiver does not mention pins in his *Brief Directions*, in a manuscript dated 1690 he did advise that 'Insects as Spiders flyes Butterflyes and Beetles' should be preserved by thrusting a pin through their body and sticking them in one's hat, until one had the opportunity to get a board and pin them to the wall of one's cabin, or the inside lid of any 'deal box', so that they would avoid being crushed.[33] The pinning of insects would become standard procedure for the arrangement and presentation of specimens in the years to follow, a tradition which served not only the interests of science but the aesthetic inclinations of collectors themselves.

The eighteenth-century Danish zoologist Johan Christian Fabricius was the most prodigious student of Carl Linnaeus (the Swedish founder of taxonomy), being once called the 'Linnaeus of insects',[34] and publishing his first zoological work, *Systema entomologiae,* in 1775. Linnaeus had identified around 3,000 insects, including 654 beetles; Fabricius, over 10,000 insects, including 4,112 beetles, between 1775 and 1801.[35] Fabricius's *Philosophia entomologica* (1778) was the first entomology textbook; here, he wrote tellingly that 'the number of species in entomology is almost infinite and if they are not brought in order entomology will always be in chaos.'[36] This passage suggests that the various improvements, modifications and refinements of Linnaeus were seen as part of a necessary defence against the omnipresent threat to rational order posed by the insects' overwhelming diversity and sheer numbers. Beetles, as the most prolific insects (about 40 per cent of all the insects discovered by Fabricius were beetles), were at the forefront of this assault. It was a challenge faced directly, if naively, by entomologists in the decades that followed, as the number of known beetle species continued to balloon.

In *A Decade of Curious Insects* (1773), John Hill proclaimed that 'we shall find throughout [nature's] universal regions, that creatures differ by equidistant steps from one another', and that 'this difference, this advance of Species above Species, is all her laws allow'. For Hill, species were a property of nature 'herself', whereas 'Classes, and Genera, tho' useful, are arbitrary; ideas of mens minds; that exist not in nature.'[37] Clearly following in the rational footsteps of Linnaeus, Hill nevertheless made the erroneous remark that 'Insects are not so numerous, as 'tis the custom now to think them.'[38] Few could have shared Hill's wishful thinking here – indeed, it was becoming ever more apparent that insects' numbers were being consistently underestimated.

German entomologists in particular seemed determined to account for every extant beetle species, with one of the first attempts to do so coming in the eighteenth century with Carl Gustav Jablonsky and Johann Friedrich Wilhelm Herbst's ten-volume *Natursystem aller bekannten in-und ausländischen Insekten: als eine Fortsetzung der von Büffonschen Naturgeschichte: nach dem System des Ritters Carl von Linné bearbeitet: Der Käfer* (Natural System of all Well-known Foreign Insects, as a Continuation of Buffon's Nautral History, After the systems of the Honoured Master Carl von Linné). With copious, finely detailed colour illustrations, including images of dissected beetles and their internal anatomy, it was published between 1785 and 1806. Following this impressive but ultimately insufficient effort, the German coleopterists Max Gemminger and Baron Edgar von Harold attempted the same task in their twelve-volume

Catalogus coleopterorum hucusque descriptorum synonymicus et sys-tematicus (Systematic catalogue of beetles that have been described to present, with their synonyms). Published between 1868 and 1876, it lists nearly 77,000 species. In the twentieth century, between 1910 and 1940, Wilhelm Junk and Sigmund Schenkling listed nearly 221,500 species in their *Coleopterorum catalogus* – this work, however, represents the last attempt to account for every species of beetle within a single volume.[39] The rate of discovery of new species, as mentioned previously, is simply too high for any such attempt to be thorough, or the results durable. In the 70 years since Junk and Schenkling's effort, around 130,000 more beetle species have been described – an average of five per day, every day – and the number continues to climb.

'Rebellious Beetles', J. J. Grandville's illustration for *Public and Private Life of Animals* (1877).

As the pursuit and cataloguing of beetles gained serious momentum in the second half of the eighteenth century, power struggles emerged as collectors competed with each other for recognition and prestige. One particularly telling example is that of William Hunter's Goliath beetle, in which disputes over 'ownership' of both the type specimen and its image arose.[40] The first specimen of the Goliath beetle (*Goliathus goliatus*) was found floating in the mouth of a Gabon river in the Gulf of Guinea, Africa, in 1766, by the captain of a merchant ship. He passed it to a navy surgeon, David Ogilvie, who then passed it to the Scottish anatomist William Hunter. At 9.5 cm (3.7 in.) long, it was one of the largest beetles yet discovered. Three years later, an image of the Goliath or zebra beetle appeared in Dru Drury's *Illustrations of Natural History* (1770), but the source of the image – that is, the specimen from which it had been drawn – remained unacknowledged. The image, engraved by the widely esteemed natural history illustrator Moses Harris, had been based on the original plate which Drury had purchased from the English botanist Emanuel Mendes da Costa, who was apparently a man of dubious honour, having been imprisoned twice for illicit financial dealings, one of which involved embezzling more than £1,100 from the Royal Society while he served as its clerk. Hunter had loaned the beetle to Mendes da Costa, who was preparing a book on natural history and wanted to include an image of the Goliath beetle rendered by his own hand. Instead, Mendes da Costa – now imprisoned and evidently desperate to raise money – had provided his own, unpublished illustration of the beetle to Drury, who then allowed Harris to copy it for inclusion in Drury's book. This seems to have greatly offended Hunter, who felt that credit ultimately owed to him had now been wrongly directed to Drury and Harris, and that da Costa had violated the conditions of the loan of the specimen. In a terse response to the long letter of apology he received from da Costa, Hunter wrote in 1771:

Illustration from Jules Michelet, *The Insect* (1883).

Dr Hunter is sorry that Mr Da Costa has taken so much trouble. It is a thing of very little consequence, but cannot be set right because it was very wrong. Mr Da Costa's owning it was wrong is enough. But it must remain so. Dr Hunter chuses no further dealings. He thinks Mr Drury likewise has behaved in a way which he should not have expected. But if they are pleased with themselves he has nothing to say.[41]

While some beetles lay at the centre of largely ego-driven disputes among gentleman naturalists, others figured in decidedly more inspirational affairs. One (possibly apocryphal) story tells

how in 1793, the prodigious French zoologist Pierre André Latreille
found himself imprisoned in the dungeons of Bordeaux, guilty of
being a member of the ecclesiastical class during the height of his
country's revolutionary turmoil. He had languished in his cell for
some time when the prison's physician decided to inspect the
inmates. At the time of the physician's visit, Latreille was pre-
occupied with an unusual beetle he had found on the floor of his
cell. The physician initially took Latreille's fixed interest in the
insect as a sign of madness, until Latreille advised that it was in
fact a very rare specimen. The physician took the beetle and delivered it to his acquaintance, Jean Baptiste Bory de Saint-Vincent, a
fifteen-year-old aspiring naturalist who was familiar with Latreille's
publications. The diminutive beetle, measuring between 4 and 6
mm (0.2 in.) in length, was indeed rare. It was *Necrobia ruficollis*,

the ham beetle. Flattered to have been involved in Latreille's entomological work, the apparently well-connected teenage naturalist was able to secure his release; within a month, all the remaining inmates were dead as violence erupted throughout the region.[42]

Perhaps the greatest figure in early nineteenth-century coleopterology was Pierre F.M.A. Dejean who, in addition to describing many beetle species and amassing one of the largest beetle collections in the world during his own time (about 20,000 specimens), also served as Napoleon's aide-de-camp during the Battle of Waterloo. He began his catalogue of beetles in 1802, and it contained more than 22,000 entries by the final edition in 1837. Dejean's dedication to beetle collecting is best exemplified by an incident that allegedly occurred on the battlefield – a most unlikely stage for a meaningful beetle encounter. During the Battle of Alcañiz, in May of 1809, Dejean was preparing to give the order to charge into the Spanish line. He then happened to notice a beetle on the ground by his horse. This was reason enough for him to delay the order, dismount, collect the beetle, pin it to some cork that he had glued inside his helmet for precisely this purpose, and only then recommence the battle. Hundreds of French soldiers died in the ensuing canon fire from the Spanish; Dejean's helmet was shattered, but both he and the beetle specimen survived. Sadly, by the time he got around to naming it, some years later, the beetle had already been found, described and recorded in a scholarly journal by another naturalist, rendering Dejean's proposed name – *Cebrio ustulatus* – superfluous, and his daring moment of battlefield entomology ultimately redundant.[43]

Obsession with natural history collections spread throughout the nineteenth century, and beetles were prominent figures in this process. Their apparently infinite diversity of form and colour continued to provide collectors with the thrill of the new, the unseen, the surprising. The European middle class that had begun to emerge in the eighteenth century continued to expand, in conjunction with an increasing desire to escape (if only temporarily) the cramped, noisy and dirty conditions of the city. For those with both the means and the inclination, natural history became something of a respite, a leisure pursuit which could nevertheless intersect with science and the accrual of knowledge about the natural world. Although a keen interest in insects of any kind was still often regarded with some disparagement in the first half of the nineteenth century, this had begun to change with the improving public profile of natural history in general, and with a growing appreciation – made all the more palpable by the relatively sudden influx of affordable microscopes – that even the smallest of nature's productions were worthy of close attention. Beetles rewarded such attention and were considered by a number of authors as exemplary of the 'insect tribe' in its entirety. Although the direct quotation of Pliny was less common in the nineteenth century, there were ongoing reverberations of this classical source; one author reminded his readers that 'The importance of organisms, singly or collectively, is not always

'Go it Charlie!' Caricature of Charles Darwin by his university friend Albert Way from 1832.

proportionate to their size, nay, is frequently to be measured in an inverse ratio.'[44]

Other authors took this line of thought further, feeling obliged to make more direct comparisons between beetles and larger, more highly valued animals. The Scottish entomologist James Duncan wrote in 1835:

> They may be said to symbolize those higher animals which are most remarkable for the perfection of their organs, and which are therefore regarded as the types of their respective classes, such as the feline race among quadrupeds, and eagles among birds . . . At the same time, the important functions which they perform in the economy of nature, and the injurious consequences which not unfrequently result to mankind from their undue diminution or increase, impart a greater degree of importance to their history than attaches to the generality of the insect tribes.[45]

Much of the nineteenth-century advance of natural history, of course, was motivated by the publication of Darwin's *On the Origin of Species* in 1859. After Darwin's theory took hold, a specimen was always more than a specimen – it was also a verified 'link' between two others already known, an indicator of evolution-in-progress.[46] The theory of natural selection situated beetles within a much grander physical system than had previously been visible in nature, rich with meaning and significant of deep time. Although Darwin is not known as an entomologist (he described himself in later years as a 'decayed entomologist'), insects in general, and beetles in particular, had played a formative role in his dedicated movement into natural history. After losing interest in the study of medicine, in 1828 he was sent by his father to Christ's College, Cambridge, to study for a Bachelor of Arts in preparation for becoming an

Anglican parson. There he met his second cousin, William Darwin Fox, who introduced the young Darwin to beetle collecting. Although Darwin had demonstrated an interest in natural history from an early age, his time chasing beetles in Cambridge seems to have lifted that interest considerably. In his autobiography, Darwin wrote:

But no pursuit at Cambridge was followed with nearly so much eagerness or gave me so much pleasure as collecting beetles. It was the mere passion for collecting, for I did not dissect them and rarely compared their external characters with published descriptions, but got them named anyhow. I will give a proof of my zeal: one day, on tearing off some old bark, I saw two rare beetles and seized one in each hand; then I saw a third and new kind, which I could not bear to lose, so that I popped the one which I held in my right hand into my mouth. Alas it ejected some intensely acrid fluid, which burnt my tongue so that I was forced to spit the beetle out, which was lost, as well as the third one.[47]

The scene described by Darwin evokes a child in a sweetshop, or perhaps Willy Wonka's chocolate factory, greedily hoarding the sweets to himself; such was the passion for the collection, not just of beetles, but of natural history 'objects' in general, that emerged prominently during the nineteenth century. Although Darwin may have avoided the unpleasantness of dissecting his specimens (he had withdrawn from medical studies for similar reasons), he was very much at ease with treating these animals as collectible objects. Within this mode, his enthusiasm for nature was inspired further still. He noted that in later years he was surprised by the indelible impression left upon his mind by many of the beetles he caught at Cambridge, and that he could remember the exact appearance of certain posts, old trees and banks where he made a good capture.[48] For Darwin, the youthful collection of beetles was inextricably tied to a sense of place. The thrill of collecting new or rare specimens was for him a feeling of sufficient intensity to form enduring and vivid memories of the specific locations where those thrills occurred.

While anecdotes such as these, drenched in nostalgia and conveying the beetle's ability to form a lasting impression incommensurate with its diminutive size, would become pervasive in much nineteenth-century entomology, human–beetle relations were not all sunshine and roses. With the rapidly expanding human population came new challenges – especially those concerning the provision and distribution of food and fibre – which cast some insects, including beetles, in an increasingly negative light. It was not enough to merely account for and collect beetle species – things would need to be *done* with this knowledge. One author noted in 1887 that 'as civilization advanced, the conviction was gaining ground more and more that knowledge of insect life was essential to continued success in agricultural and other pursuits.'[49]

In a paradox that would become increasingly pronounced into the twentieth century and beyond, the more Western civilization 'advanced' – the more it 'elevated' itself and its members from the trials, burdens and dangers of nature – the more entwined with beetles did its fate become.

4 Managing Beetles

Little wrongs have to be done, in order that greater wrongs may be avoided. If I kill a Colorado beetle, I do wrong by the beetle; but, if I fail to kill it, I do wrong by all the growers and consumers of potatoes, and their interests are vastly more important.
A. M. MacIver, *Ethics and the Beetle*[1]

Globally, about half of all food and fibre produced is lost to field and storage 'pests' – insects, pathogens, nematodes, weeds and vertebrates.[2] Although the contribution of insects to this decimation is difficult to measure accurately, most estimates place it between 10 and 15 per cent. Beetles certainly play their part here, and numerous examples will be provided in the pages that follow. But in order to understand the kind of relationship a beetle 'pest' has with human beings, we must clarify what is meant by 'pest' in the first instance. The most widely agreed upon definition of an insect pest is 'any insect in the wrong place – from a human point of view . . . Thus any insect may be a pest under one set of conditions, and not so under others.'[3] This makes a particular beetle's status as pest entirely contingent upon human concerns, and hence subject to change. Rather than 'making pests of themselves', it is we who make pests of beetles.

Beetles have hindered human interests for millennia, to varying degrees. But the scale, nature and consistency of this hindrance have dramatically increased in modern times, especially with the advent of large-scale agriculture. Our ever-expanding global population has come to rely on vulnerable monocrops for much of its food and fibre. In his classic of natural history, *The Natural History and Antiquities of Selborne* (1789), Gilbert White signalled the emerging concern with insect pests as major threats to food and fibre crops and stores. In the late eighteenth century, the systematic study of insects was in a comparatively early stage, and was yet to break off into specialized subdisciplines, such as agricultural and economic entomology. White wrote that a full history of noxious insects in the field, garden and house would certainly prove a useful and important work, and that what knowledge there was of that sort lay scattered and unorganized. Should such a work be assembled, great improvements would soon follow.[4] White recognized, perhaps implicitly, that with the looming emergence of mass production and global trade amid the British agricultural revolution, insects posed new kinds of threats – put plainly, the more food and fibre humans produced, the more there was to be damaged and destroyed by insects. But he was also attentive to more local circumstances, noting that an insect that infested turnips and numerous garden crops, which the country people called the 'turnip-fly' or 'black-dolphin', was actually one of the Coleoptera, and that during very hot summers they abounded to such a degree that they would make a pattering sound like rain when jumping on the leaves of turnips and cabbages.[5]

Colorado potato beetle (*Leptinotarsa decemlineata*).

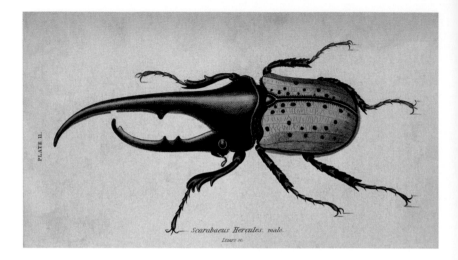

PLATE II.

Scarabaeus Hercules. male.

Lizars sc.

Amale scarabaeus, coloured engraving by W. H. Lizars (1788–1859).

By 1853 the Scottish naturalist Sir William Jardine was able to report, in his edited reissue of White's *Natural History*, that 'Many good papers have been published upon the insects injurious to the husbandman and gardener, and the Messrs. Loudon and Westwood have translated Keller's German treatise upon "Noxious Insects".'[6] Yet there was still much to be done in this field – indeed, the management and prevention of insect pests, including beetles, was to become a permanent and increasingly complex concern around the world. In his *Farm Insects* of 1860, John Curtis worried that while chemistry and geology had been so valuable in rendering the land more fertile, little attention had comparatively been paid to 'those noxious animals' which annually consume an incalculable amount of produce.[7]

Valid concerns about the destruction of crops were, by the second half of the nineteenth century, becoming increasingly bound up with concerns about 'foreign species' in the broadest sense. As industrialized Western nations expanded and developed their own territories, not only did they inevitably cross paths with foreign species, but they facilitated the movement of those species into new areas. These inadvertently assisted migrations could threaten essential crops and human welfare, but they could also provoke widespread cultural fears of imminent, nascent threats of an equally symbolic degree, not entirely dissimilar to the post-9/11 fear of terrorist 'cells', the 'creeping tide' of immigration, or previous panics about 'Mad Cow Disease'.

One particularly vivid example of this modern entomophobia is the case of the Colorado beetle, or Colorado potato beetle (*Leptinotarsa decemlineata*). First described in 1824 by the eminent American entomologist Thomas Say, the Colorado potato beetle averages 10 mm (0.4 in.) in length, exhibiting bright yellow and orange elytra marked with brown stripes. Although now thought to be a native of Mexico, it seemed to live primarily in Colorado, feeding discreetly on indigenous buffalo bur (a grassy weed), until the 1850s. At some point during that decade, however, the westward migration of speculative miners inadvertently introduced the Colorado beetle to the potato plant. A reliable staple crop on the

A student from Amargosa Valley elementary school in Nevada examines an *Eleodes* beetle caught in a pitfall trap.

frontier, the potato plant also proved highly accommodating to the beetle's life cycle, and soon became its preferred alternative to buffalo bur. So voracious was the Colorado beetle's appetite for the haulm and leaves of the potato plant that it undertook 'a relentless seventy-mile-a-year march towards the Atlantic. By 1874 it had brought its masticating mania to the Atlantic Seaboard,' extending its population range by more than one mile per week for twenty consecutive years.[8] In 1876 the *New York Times* reported from Grinnell Station that the railway was covered with them for a mile, and that after a few revolutions, the wheels lost friction and slipped as if oiled. The beetles had to be swept off, and the track sanded, before any progress could be made.[9]

Understandably, this sudden, public explosion of an unfamiliar pest capable of decimating potato plants led to some trepidation, not only in the United States, but in the United Kingdom, where memories of the potato famine (1846–51) were still fresh in the minds of many. Ireland had seen at least 1 million people die, and another million emigrate, as a direct result of dependence on a single staple, which had failed after being overwhelmed by a lowly fungus (*Phytophthora infestans*). Although it was clear, at least to American entomologists, that neither the Colorado beetle nor its larvae would be transported with potatoes themselves (the insect is attracted only to the haulm and leaves, which are not shipped with the tubers), almost all agreed that if the insect found its way to Britain, it would do so in its perfect, highly resilient adult form. So resilient was the adult beetle, in fact, that it could potentially survive a transatlantic sea voyage – aboard any ship it happened upon – without any form of sustenance whatsoever. The only way to ensure a complete blockade of the beetle in Britain, according to the British Chamber of Agriculture, was to enforce a prohibition of all North American imports – potatoes, and everything else.[10]

W. Raddon after the Rev. L. Guilding of a sugar cane boring beetle, showing the adult, pupa and larva stages, 19th-century etching.

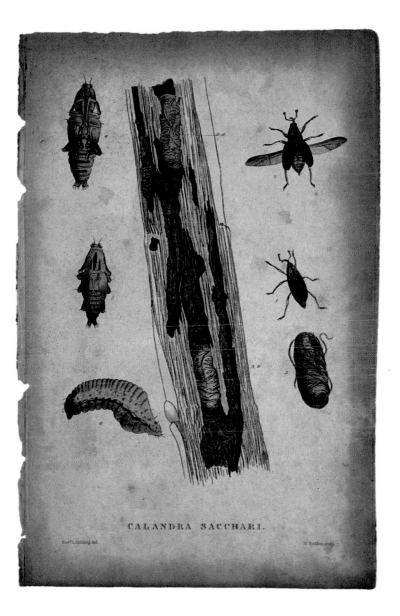

CALANDRA SACCHARI.

Although Germany, France, Russia, the Netherlands and Spain chose to restrict or prohibit the importation of American potatoes, by 1875 around 50 per cent of Britain's wheat supply was necessarily imported – much of it from the United States. Despite the implorations of (newly emergent) agricultural entomologists, the British government did not deem the termination of all American imports to be a viable option. What was an option, however, was the drafting of some of the earliest insect legislation in Europe – the Destructive Insects Act of 1877 – which gave the Privy Council the right to restrict or prohibit the landing of potatoes, haulms, leaves or any other article that might introduce the Colorado beetle to Great Britain, and to remove or destroy any crop suspected of sheltering the beetle or of promoting its spread. A combination of diligence and good fortune meant that the Colorado beetle never did invade Britain, and the Act was evoked only once, in 1901, upon an infested plot of potatoes in Tilbury.[11]

However, elsewhere the Colorado beetle remains a serious and persistent pest to potato crops, as well as a menace to tomatoes and aubergines (eggplants). Inadvertently introduced to Western Europe during the First World War, it is now well established in all of Europe except the British Isles, and continues to expand east and south through Eastern Europe and Asia.[12] In 1950 the Soviet Union launched a propaganda campaign blaming the United States Air Force for East Germany's Colorado potato beetle problem. Diminishing potato supplies were a serious concern in Germany, where reliance on this staple was (and remains) high. According to the Soviet Zone's Office of Information, the beetles had been systematically dropped from the air on the night of 24 May 1950. An 'official map' was published, showing the American bomber's route over the state of Saxony. Hence declining potato supplies in East Germany were the direct result of an American offensive, rather than domestic mismanagement. On 6 July, the u.s. Department of State replied:

It is interesting to note that the Soviet propagandists have borrowed this whole invention from the Nazis who during the war used to level the same fantastic charge against Allied airplanes . . . The facts – of which the Soviet government was undoubtedly aware when making its charge – are that potato bugs, or Colorado beetles, have existed in Germany since before the war; have been spreading rapidly in wartime due to absence of effective counter measures; and were recognized as a serious threat to the East-zone economy by the eastern German puppet government several months prior to the date of the alleged American bug offensive.[13]

Downgraded to a minor pest in the first half of the twentieth century as a result of the successful deployment of chemical insecticides, the Colorado potato beetle developed a resistance to DDT in the 1950s, and has since proven highly resistant to all subsequent attempts at chemical control.

Cotton, as a modern, global monocrop, has also had its fair share of beetle trouble, particularly in the United States. Introduced to Florida in 1556, it was sown in Jamestown, Virginia, by British colonists upon their arrival there in 1607. Throughout the colonial period, cotton was grown on a modest scale, but increasing demand from Britain led to the invention of spinning and weaving machines in the second half of the eighteenth century. In turn, this required improved methods for growing cotton and preparing the raw fibre, to fully exploit the new output potential of the machines. Eli Whitney's invention of the cotton gin in 1793, which allowed for rapid separation of the seed from the fibre of short-staple cotton (thus preparing the fibre for spinning), is usually considered the beginning of the modern cotton industry, and American production increased exponentially soon thereafter – albeit remaining heavily

Imperishable insects created by scientists. William R. Walton, Senior Entomologist of the Division of Cereal and Forage Insects, u.s. Department of Agriculture, 1937.

'Beat the Boll Weevil' educational bulletin published by the U.S. Food Administration Educational Division in 1918.

reliant on human slavery to ensure maximum profits for landowners and investors. By 1860 the United States was producing two-thirds of the world's supply of cotton, generating unprecedented wealth in the South.[14]

Enter the boll weevil (*Anthonomus grandis*), a dark, grey-brown beetle native to Central America and Mexico, averaging 6 mm (0.2 in.) in length with a prominent snout, who lives, feeds and reproduces upon the cotton plant. The boll weevil crossed the Rio Grande from Mexico into Texas around 1892, and within 30 years had spread throughout the entire cotton-growing region of the South, devastating crops and bringing financial ruin to plantation owners and workers alike. Floods in 1915 and 1916 destroyed much of what the boll weevil had left in its wake,[15] and by 1922 up to 85 per cent of the Cotton Belt had been infested as the weevil proceeded up the Atlantic Seaboard. Although the spread of the boll weevil and its impoverishment of cotton plantations throughout the South has been seen as a primary cause of the northward 'Great Migration' of African Americans, the migration and the boll weevil actually spread in opposite directions. While the boll weevil was making its way up through Texas, African Americans in Florida and the southeast were beginning to move northward. Migration fever moved from east to west, while the 'march of the boll weevil' was from west to east.[16]

The boll weevil left its indelible mark on folk culture, too. The pioneering American folklorist and musicologist John A. Lomax documented many local variants of the 'Ballet of the Boll Weevil', a song devised and performed by black plantation workers in the first decade of the twentieth century. Using language very much indicative of its time, he wrote that:

> The negroes have made a song about the invasion of the boll-weevil, the destruction it has wrought, and the efforts

of entomologists to subdue it. Just as they sympathize with the weaker and the shrewder Brer Rabbit against his stronger opponents Brer Fox and Brer Wolf, so do the negroes in the 'Ballet of the Boll-Weevil' sympathize with the puny boll-weevil against the attacks of the white man. There are perhaps one hundred stanzas to this song, and new ones turn up in every community of negroes I visit.[17]

However problematic Lomax's phrasing may appear to the present reader, his basic interpretation – that the plantation workers were expressing an affinity with the beetle – was an accurate one. One of the most widely repeated stanzas reads:

Well, the boll weevil is a little black bug
Come from Mexico they say
Well he come all the way to Texas
He was lookin' for a place to stay
Just lookin' for a home,
He was lookin' for a home.

The repetition of the 'just lookin' for a home' passage runs throughout most versions of the song, being particularly pronounced in the chorus; and as Lomax noted:

The concluding stanza of this ballad, which is certainly the product of unlettered negroes, runs as follows:-
'If anybody axes you who wuz it writ dis song,
Tell 'em it wuz a dark-skinned nigger
Wid a pair of blue duckins on
A-lookin' fur a home,
Jes a-lookin' fur a home.'[18]

Lomax's son, Alan Lomax, also an accomplished collector of folk music in the field, recorded a particularly famous version, 'Boll Weevil Blues', performed by Lead Belly in 1934. In 1943, defending the ballad against a critic who remarked that it had 'nothing in common with "good" ballads . . . It is very much what we should expect of a song which emerged from unlettered negroes,' another American folklorist with his heart (if not his words) in the right place responded: 'Unlike Professor Pound, I expect good ballads from unlettered Negroes and get them often,' further noting that the song has a subtlety about it. The song recognizes that the weevil needs a place to live, and plays with the idea that if the weevil gets a home, man may no longer have one; it has a humorous tone, derived from the fact that the fate of the cotton crops is not quite as important to those who labour on them as it is to those who sell them.[19] The song seemed to have been written by plantation hands who identified with the 'black little bug', and certainly sympathized with him.[20] Versions of the song continued to emerge throughout the twentieth century, from artists as diverse as Woody Guthrie, Eddie Cochran, Patti Page, Brook Benton (for whom it was a major hit), Shocking Blue, The White Stripes, and even Australian children's entertainers The Wiggles.

A very localized cultural response to the boll weevil is found in the city of Enterprise, Alabama (population approximately 25,000). Like much of the South, it had invested heavily in cotton, but was visited by the boll weevil in 1915, with predictable results. Within a very short amount of time almost 60 per cent of the county's cotton crops were destroyed, forcing farmers to turn to alternatives – primarily, peanuts. By 1917, just two years after the arrival of the rapacious boll weevil, the county was harvesting more peanuts than any other in the United States, and was liberated from the monocrop system of 'King Cotton'. Residents acknowledged the boll weevil's part in this fortuitous turnaround, and subsequently

Boll weevil monument, Enterprise, Alabama.

Cantharidine is a substance secreted from a type of beetle commonly known as the Spanish fly. It was used as a counter-irritant, the technique being to irritate one part of the body, raising blisters on the skin, in order to relieve it in another.

erected the world's first (and only) public monument to an agricultural pest, dedicated in 1919. A classical female beauty holding a large boll weevil above her head, it stands in the centre of the downtown district, its base bearing the inscription: 'In profound appreciation of the boll weevil and what it has done as the herald of prosperity this monument was erected by the citizens of Enterprise, Coffee County, Alabama.'[21] Few other cities shared the good fortune of Enterprise, but since the initiation of the U.S. Department of Agriculture's Boll Weevil Eradication programme in 1978, which incorporates pheromone traps, reduction of the weevil's food supply and chemical control, more than 80 per cent of the boll weevil population has been removed from the 6 million ha (15 million acres) dedicated to cotton crops in the United States.[22]

In the incessant and apparently permanent 'war against insects', beetles have sometimes served as our friends, rather than foes. Perhaps the greatest (human) success story in the history of insect pest control is that of the vedalia beetle (*Rodolia cardinalis*), a species of ladybird native to Australia that became instrumental in the salvation of the Californian citrus industry. In 1887, this industry was in its early stages, but the potential for large-scale success was apparent. California growers, however, were beleaguered by an infestation of cottony cushion scale (*Icerya purchasi*), a species of bug (order Hemiptera). Charles Valentine Riley, an entomologist for the United States Department of Agriculture (USDA) and Chief of the Division of Entomology, spoke that year to the concerned Fruit Growers' Association in Riverside, California. Although Riley knew the cottony cushion scale was from Australasia, he was unsure whether it had originated from Australia or New Zealand (it had

Ladybird larva feeding on an aphid.

accidentally been introduced to New Zealand from Australia in the nineteenth century), and he believed it had arrived in California on acacia (probably kangaroo acacia, *Acacia paradoxa*) imported to Menlo Park in 1868.

Riley was known as an aggressive problem solver, rigorously promoting the importance of agricultural entomology and the need for its widespread institution in the United States. With very little delay, he sent a field agent to Australia, the naturalized German immigrant Albert Koebele. Arriving in August of 1888, Koebele's mission was to identify natural enemies of the cottony cushion scale in the field, with a view to bringing them back to California. By October of that year, he had identified the dipterous parasite *Cryptochaetum iceryae* (a fly), and three predaceous larvae: a *Chrysopa* (lacewing) species, and two larvae of a *Coccinella*. The *Coccinella* were the vedalia beetles, which Koebele had found feeding on the cottony cushion scale in a North Adelaide garden, in South Australia.

Koebele sent three shipments of the beetles to his colleague in Los Angeles, Daniel W. Coquillet, between November 1889 and

Valley elderberry longhorn beetle (*Desmocerus californicus dimorphus*a).

'Digging for Beetles', in Jean-Henri Fabre, *La Vie des insectes* (1920).

January 1890: 129 specimens in total. The beetles were placed under a tent on an infested orange tree at the J. W. Wolfskill ranch in Los Angeles, which thus became the first insectary in California. Allowed to live and breed undisturbed, they proceeded to quickly and efficiently demolish the cottony cushion scale. In April, they were introduced to adjoining trees within the orchard, where previous results were repeated. In a bold and perhaps overly optimistic decision, Coquillet then began distributing vedalia beetles throughout the state: by June of 1890 he had sent 10,555 of them to 228 orchardists. The results were repeated widely, apparently with no adverse effects, and within one year shipments of oranges from Los Angeles County increased from 700 to 2,000 carloads.[23] In

1929 Los Angeles County's annual horticultural report noted that there were 103 workers on the payroll raising beneficial insects, including 6 million lady beetles that were distributed over 4,450 ha (11,000 acres).[24] The importation of the vedalia beetle was a dramatic triumph of modern methods of biological control, and today (along with the parasitic fly, *Cryptochetum iceryae*) the beetle continues to keep cottony cushion scale numbers low, and citrus production high.

While Australia was providing benevolent beetles to the United States, however, it was facing a looming beetle battle of its own. The cultivation of sugar cane emerged as a viable industry there in the mid-1860s; beginning in southern Queensland, it spread north through the coastal plains and river valleys to Mossman in the far north, and south to Grafton in northern New South Wales. Currently, Australia is the third largest supplier of raw sugar in the world, exporting 80 per cent of its annual yield of 4.5–5 million tonnes, at a value of $1.5–$2.5 billion. But in 1872, less than ten years after cane farming began, growers in Mackay, Queensland, 970 km (602 miles) north of Brisbane, reported severe damage to crops by white grubs – the larvae of 'cane beetles', a collective term for a variety of beetles especially fond of sugar cane. There were more attacks in the Herbert, Johnstone and Cairns districts through the 1880s, but not of a scale sufficient to provoke alarm. However, in the mid-1890s widespread losses were incurred in the Mackay, Herbert, Johnstone and Isis districts, and farmers began to fear for their businesses. At this point the matter became a concern for the state government, which had promoted cane farming as a worthwhile opportunity for European settlers in the tropical, and often harsh, Queensland climate. Lobbying by sugar millers and cane growers eventually persuaded the Queensland Bureau of Sugar Experiment Stations (BSES) to hire an entomologist in 1911 and establish a Division of Entomology. During the next four decades,

Illustration from Johann Eusebius Voet and Georg Wolfgang Franz Panzer, *Johann Euseb Voets Beschreibungen und Abbildungen hartschaaligter Insekten, Coleoptera Linn . . .* (1793).

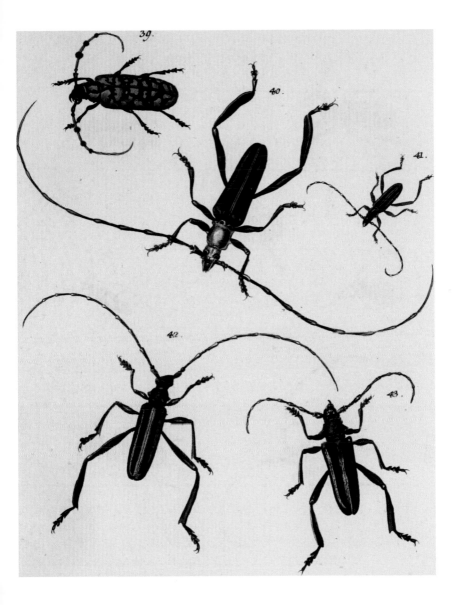

more entomologists became involved with the Division, focusing on the biology of the cane beetles and determining methods to combat them.[25]

In 1917 Edmund Jarvis, one of Queensland's earliest entomologists and employee of the Queensland BSES, vividly described the evening flight of the cane beetles, an event almost impossible to avoid in the cane-growing regions during the tropical summer months:

> Standing among the cane stools, one seems to be encompassed by an immense swarm of beetles – thousands being in view at the one time – which, in their erratic and ill-directed flight, are constantly striking against the cane leaves, the clapping noise produced by the sudden impact being plainly audible at a distance of several yards. In addition to this oft-repeated sound, the air, so still before, vibrates loudly with a continuous hum, due to the accumulated buzzing of countless numbers of these insects.[26]

Various attempts at chemical control failed to stem the tide of the cane beetles. In early 1935 Reginald W. Mungomery assumed control of the district around Meringa, between Gordonvale and Cairns in North Queensland, charged with the task of solving the beetle problem. Mungomery was aware of the success the Puerto Rican sugarcane industry had achieved in using the giant American toad (*Bufo marinus*), which fed on cane beetle species in South America. The toads had already been introduced to Hawaii and the Philippines in 1932 and 1934 to control cane beetles, and Mungomery decided to follow suit in Australia. Although Mungomery didn't explain his reasoning, he may have been frustrated with the pace of investigations under Jarvis's direction, especially the cautious testing of the impact of control measures.[27]

In June 1935 Mungomery travelled to Hawaii and returned with 102 giant American toads, 51 male and 51 female. These were released into a dedicated pond in Meringa, where they reproduced rapidly. Later that year, more toads were released in the Cairns and Innisfail districts, but by the end of 1935 the Commonwealth Director-General of Health prohibited the release of more toads, concerned that they 'might eradicate insects of economic value'.[28] It was clear that important questions about the environmental consequences of introducing the toads to Queensland had not been asked, let alone resolved. However, the ban was lifted in September of 1936, and toads were released into sugar-producing districts along the Queensland coast as far south as Bundaberg.[29]

It quickly became apparent, however, that the introduction of the giant American toad was a blunder of considerable proportions. All the cautious testing that characterized previous investigations into cane grub control methods was completely forgotten when it came to the cane toad, and there seems to be no sign of any pre-release testing by the BSES entomologists to confirm that the toads

A greyback cane beetle larva infected with the fungi metarhizium, the active ingredient in the biopesticide Bio-Cane.

even ate the cane beetles.[30] By 1939 the BSES reported that the 'number of toads present in the field was insufficient to effect a material reduction in the pest'.[31] Investigations of toad stomach contents showed that some toads had begun to gorge on the beetles, yet it was painfully obvious that the number of toads required to significantly reduce beetle swarms was unrealistic. From 1939 onwards, no further mention of the effectiveness of the toad appears in BSES reports.[32]

Although the 'cane toad' (as it has become known in Australia) is considered an icon in Queensland, an animal mascot of state identity, it remains a serious pest throughout the state and beyond. Continuing to spread southwards and westwards across the continent, it currently occupies 50 per cent of Queensland and small portions of New South Wales and the Northern Territory,

George Bornemissza and dung beetles, which he introduced to Australia in 1967. The beetles break down the cow pads which previously had covered valuable grazing land and provided a breeding ground for flies.

an area of 1.2 million sq. km (460,000 square miles).[33] When traumatized, the toad will eject a toxic fluid from glands located on the sides of its head, making it deadly to many species of native fauna that have not had time to adapt to the presence of such an unfamiliar animal. The cane beetle, meanwhile, remains a formidable foe for the sugar cane industry in Australia; it was widely controlled with the chemical insecticide 'gammexane' (benzene hexachloride, now known to be carcinogenic) from 1947, but this was prohibited in 1987 after traces of the substance were found in exported foodstuffs other than sugar. New insecticides, integrated pest management strategies and the breeding of resistant cane varieties that either kill grubs or slow their development are now in place throughout Queensland.[34]

The reproduction, movement and spread of pests are often referred to as 'invasions', but such a term risks misrepresenting the phenomenon at hand. More specifically, the term 'invasive species' often establishes an aggressive agency for the non-human species, and a passive innocence for the human beings affected. While this may help us to make sense of very complex interspecies relationships, it does so at the expense of relevant details, and permits the misdirected attribution of blame. Contemporary representations of the mountain pine beetle (*Dendroctonus ponderosae*) exemplify this process quite vividly, and say much about our willingness and ability to disavow the extent to which our own interests and actions create the 'pests' themselves.

The mountain pine beetle is native to the pine forests of North America; it is dark grey-brown in colour, and averages 5 mm (0.2 in.) in length. It is currently at the centre of the largest infestation of British Columbian pine forests in recorded history, but extends beyond that region into Colorado, Wyoming, Nebraska and South Dakota. In Colorado and Wyoming, the beetle has impacted more than 1.6 million ha (4 million acres) since the outbreak began in

1996. Its primary host in British Columbia is the mature (over 60 years old) lodgepole pine tree (*Pinus contorta*). Adults arrive on the lodgepole pines during the summer, and proceed to bore through the outer bark to create vertical galleries in the inner bark. While boring the galleries, the beetles produce pheromones which attract other beetles to the site. Eggs are laid in the galleries, which produce larvae who then proceed to feed on the inner bark. At epidemic levels, this process can significantly disrupt the flow of water and nutrients within the tree, killing it. Enough trees are now being routinely killed by mountain pine beetles that salvage logging has become an established part of British Columbia's pine timber industry.[35] Campers and drivers are routinely warned about the dangers of falling trees – once killed by the beetles, trees can fall without warning.

The mountain pine beetle population in British Columbia has historically been regulated by two factors: sudden cold snaps of −30° to −40°C in early winter, causing high larval mortality, and the frequent fire interval (80–125 years) limiting the numbers of the beetle's primary host, the lodgepole pine. The cold snaps have not occurred in central British Columbia for 30 years (possibly indicative of climate change), and aggressive firefighting programmes over the last 50 years have guaranteed an abundance of lodgepole pine hosts, facilitating a population explosion of mountain pine beetles.[36] Human beings have thus directly and indirectly contributed to the current state of infestation.

As V. Haynes has observed, the visual, emotive rhetoric that has manifested around the mountain pine beetle in British Columbia lacks an explicit, rational argument. Instead, residents are told how to feel and what to believe about the beetle (and therefore the

Anti-Turkish propaganda published by the French depicting the Sultan as a beetle pinned down by a long sword, c. 1912.

crisis as a whole), rather than what to think about it.[37] A shared unwillingness to acknowledge forest mismanagement as a contributing factor in the beetle saga results in emotional and irrational representations of the beetle itself as a malicious, alien enemy. A number of local portrayals, including a CTV television commercial which aligns 'pure forest' and 'pure family' as the conjoined, innocent victims of the destructive beetle, along with an exhibit at the Royal British Columbia Museum, misrepresent the situation. As Haynes has documented, visitors moving down the hallway towards the beetle exhibit are presented with a blazing panorama accompanied by sound effects such as sirens, helicopters and the crackling of the mountainside consumed by flame. Then, the mountain pine beetle is presented, magnified to 100 times its actual size, making it seem even more dominant, destructive and alien. The title of the beetle exhibit is 'Beetle Mania', which implicitly draws an association between the insect and the band. One may assume that the correlation is meant to be between the outbreak of the beetle infestation and the contagious spread of the Fab Four's popularity, but such an association does not engender any affection towards the beetle. On the contrary, the active demonization of the mountain pine beetle gives visitors a scapegoat onto which they can displace blame for forest mismanagement, to the ultimate detriment of the very forest they hope to save.[38]

Portrayals like these, even when offered by authoritative, credible institutions such as public museums, ultimately have more in common with the twentieth-century tradition of insect propaganda than with public education. Indeed, commercial promotions of chemical insecticides and the portrayal of insect pests have often borrowed heavily from the representational conventions of war propaganda, particularly in their depictions of 'the enemy'.[39] It is also worth noting that the new roles for entomologists, in the face of insect pests, also facilitated a new, militarized role for 'science' in the twentieth century, one that could adjust to global concerns of the post-war era. *The Science News-letter* provided a clear example of this shift in 1964, in an article titled 'War Against Insects':

> Our grandchildren may never see a cockroach, a Japanese beetle or a corn earworm. The pests may all be wiped out by new scientific weapons, deadly to insects, safe for humans . . . Insect experts, called entomologists, are fighting a research war on six fronts . . .[40]

There are many more examples of beetle pests that could be included here, if space permitted. Each has its own story, and each reveals much about the complex interspecies relationships humans have formed, and continue to form, with beetles. The larger grain borer (*Prostephanus truncatus*), for example, has been a pest of stored maize in Central America for many decades, but in 1981 was identified as a new pest in Tanzania. Since that time it has spread widely throughout Africa, where dependency on maize is often a matter of life and death, and access to sophisticated pest control measures may be comparatively limited. The Asian long-horned beetle (*Anoplophora glabripennis*) was inadvertently introduced to North America during the 1980s, probably in wooden packing crates shipped from China; a voracious wood feeder, it has damaged 40 per cent of China's poplar plantations (about 2.4 million ha, or 5.9 million acres), and 35 per cent of urban trees in the United States are considered at risk of infestation.[41] Although it had been eradicated from New Jersey, Staten Island and Manhattan, and seemed to be in retreat elsewhere in the surrounding districts, the Asian long-horned beetle has recently resurfaced in Long Island, provoking the u.s. Department of Agriculture to increase staff in order to eradicate it once and for all. Globally, museums must maintain eternal vigilance against the museum beetle (*Anthrenus museorum*), whose larvae feed on animal keratin (found in fur, feathers and wool) and hence are a threat to many valuable museum collections. Ultimately, however, our conception of beetles as pests – while anchored by the real damage and destruction they cause – is an inevitable result of an increasingly globalized human society; a reminder, perhaps, that in our attempts to elevate ourselves from the natural world with technologies of agriculture and transportation, we merely embed ourselves ever more deeply within it.

An especially unsettling illustration of our increasingly intimate yet strangely detached relationship with beetles is provided by the most experimental arm of the U.S. Department of Defense, DARPA (Defense Advanced Research Projects Agency). While this example does involve the management of beetles, it has nothing to do with improving agriculture or reducing disease; at least, not yet. In March 2006, DARPA released a public solicitation for expressions of interest in its new project, titled Hybrid Insect Micro Electro-Mechanical Systems, or HI-MEMS for short. What DARPA sought were 'innovative proposals to develop technology to create insect-cyborgs, possibly enabled by intimately integrating microsystems within insects, during their early stages of metamorphosis'.[42] The Defense Department had, for reasons unclear, decided to fuse microchips with insect brain tissue (as it turned out, primarily beetles) while the insect was still growing. This would literally integrate the insect's brain with the embedded microcircuitry, thus producing what could only be referred to as an insect-cyborg. These beast-machines, it was hoped, could then be controlled remotely, or via GPS, much like the increasingly deployed UAV or 'drone' aircraft.

Convergent lady beetles (*Hippodamia convergens*), common in North America.

Responses from the entomological community were mixed, but mostly pessimistic. Few believed it was possible to effectively hijack a beetle's brain, driven as fiercely as beetles are by basic instincts. What's more, this all sounded like the stuff of science

fiction, something from a creepy, *Terminator*-style future. And yet, in January 2008, less than two years after DARPA's initial solicitation, the first direct control of insect flight by manipulating the wing motion via microprobes and electronics introduced to the brain during early metamorphosis was demonstrated. The following year saw the first report of radio control of a cyborg beetle in free flight: the system involved a radio-frequency receiver assembly, a microbattery and a live giant flower beetle (*Mecynorrhina polyphemus* or *Mecynorrhina torquata*). Flight commands were wirelessly transferred to the beetle via software named 'BeetleCommander v1.0' through a USB/Serial interface. This was a shockingly proficient feat of cybernetics, but it also seemed like the product of a very expensive and slightly deranged kind of science kit. The sense that this project may represent a 'toying' with nature emerged in a video interview with key researcher Michel Maharbiz: explaining the remote control of an elephant beetle (*Megasoma elephas*), he tapped a dormant (or possibly dead) specimen with a pencil, remarking that 'it sounds like a helicopter when it flies, it's pretty cute.'[43]

Certainly the idea of hijacking a beetle's brain in order to control its locomotion is a culturally idiosyncratic one – most cultures will not seek to do this, not just because they can't afford to, but because it does not accord with their ideas about how humans and beetles should coexist and interact. But the view of beetles as playthings is surprisingly prolific across many societies, even those who lack annual military budgets in excess of half a trillion dollars. Beetles don't have a voice, and hence they can't say no. If they suffer, it is usually imagined to be a kind of suffering so much apart from human suffering that it can barely be called suffering at all. Why shouldn't we treat them as little robots? After all, they behave very much as if they are 'pre-programmed' for specific tasks.

The problem, naturally, is that beetles are not robots. And so any attempt to treat them as if they are robots will not only do them

Current Biology

Remote-Controlled
Insect Flight

Cover of *Current Biology*, showing a flower beetle fitted with a micro-electro-mechanical system (March 2015).

a disservice, but will also leave us further unable to acknowledge their mysteries. A 1996 study of rhinoceros beetles, aimed at testing their load-carrying abilities on treadmills, hypothesized that they would have metabolic rates in direct proportion to the total load. The beetles could sustain a constant speed with loads of more than 30 times their body mass – quite an impressive feat. Yet the metabolic cost of moving a gram of additional load was more than five times cheaper than moving a gram of their body mass. This phenomenon cannot be explained by conventional models that link the biomechanics and metabolic energy cost of locomotion.[44] In other words, the rhinoceros beetles should not be able to do what they're doing. It's not clear how the beetles can bear such enormous artificial loads so much more economically than their own weight. One of the lessons to be taken from such discoveries, perhaps, is that beetles are not made in factories, standardized according to a plan. They emerge instead from the much more nebulous ecosystem of Earth itself, along with everything else, including us. There is much about beetles we still do not understand, and pretending they are robots, while opening up certain avenues of investigation, will close others down. Perhaps the desire to see beetles as if they are machines says more about the extent to which our own society, along with its members, has itself become aligned with machines.

THIS is the BEETLE, –
with her thread and needle.

5 Popular Beetle

Belonging to the scarab beetle subfamily Dynastinae, the rhinoceros beetle is perhaps one of the most enigmatic and well-known of all beetle species. Large, black and dramatically horned (though the females lack horns), the males are known for their often theatrical clashes in settling rivalries over females, provoking comparisons with the much larger mammals. The genus *Xylotrupes*, in particular, is found throughout Southeast Asia and Australia. Individuals typically reach 60 mm (2.4 in.) in length, and are easily identified by their two horns, one at the top of the head and the other extending underneath from the thorax. Each horn is slightly forked at the end, and the beetle is able to pinch them together, though without very much force. When perturbed, they will emit a surprisingly loud hiss by rubbing their abdomens against their wing sheaths, a defence mechanism which can sound very intimidating, perhaps because it triggers an ancient, unconscious memory of the snake. But all this ferocity is merely a ruse; the beetle is quite harmless to humans and can be handled safely.

In the villages of northern Thailand, the rhinoceros beetle, known locally as *kwang*, has become bound up with a unique cultural tradition: staged beetle battles in which human 'coaches' bring their well-trained prize fighters into the gambling arena, where the winner takes all. The males are tied with string to the peeled-back stalks of sugar cane, on which they sit and feed quite

'This is the Beetle with her Thread and Needle': design by Richard Wynn Keene or Dykwynkyn (1809–1887) for a pantomime character, c. 1860.

Textile incorporating iridescent elytra of the jewel beetle *Sternocera aequisignata*, Madras, India, c. 1880.

comfortably until duty calls. A hollow bamboo log serves as the battleground; inside is placed a female of the same species, who releases pheromones thought to trigger the males' fight mode. Each fighting beetle is placed at opposite ends of the log. The players then utilize a combination of direct prodding and an intriguing method of vibrational signals to coax their beetles into performance – small, notched styluses are rolled across the bamboo log to 'communicate' with the beetles, though precisely how (or to what extent) this technique works remains unclear. The log itself can be rotated at certain junctures during the battle, such as when the beetles begin to slip off the side, or when one beetle is at an advantage. The beetles will typically attempt to position their lower horn underneath their opponents, which then allows them to pinch, lift and throw them off the log. At the end of a round, players will often pick up their beetle and shake it vigorously before placing it back on the log; this seems to function as a kind of 'reset' button which usually reorients the beetle to begin the battle all over again, apparently erasing its memory of the preceding events.

Although beetle battles may be appreciated worldwide, Asian cultures seem to reserve a special fondness for them. In 2003 the video game company Sega released *Kontyu Ouja Mushi King* in arcades throughout Japan. The game (*King of Coleoptera: Bug King*, or simply *Mushi-King*) involves a variety of collectible playing cards (856 in total) which are dispensed by vending machines and inserted into the arcade consoles to assist players in various beetle battles. But the scenario depicted is not one in which heavily armed human warriors battle a swarming, relentless and alien insectoid foe (this would come in 2011, with D3Publisher's *Earth Defense Force: Insect Armageddon*). Rather, *Mushi-King* is *Street Fighter* – with an entomological, ecological message. Real beetle species are depicted, and their staged battles (involving various 'combo moves') form part of a grand narrative about protecting the forest from destruction. Soon after its initial success in arcades *Mushi-King* was released for other platforms, including Nintendo's handheld Game Boy Advance and Sony's PlayStation, adapted for an animated film, and formed the basis of tournaments across the country. By 2005 Sega had sold 256 million *Mushi-King* cards, at 100 yen (about one u.s. dollar) each, and installed 13,500 machines in 5,200 locations across Japan.[1] This popularity extended to the Philippines, Singapore and Taiwan, where variants of the arcade game also appeared. *Mushi-King* was even incorporated by Japan Airlines, who decorated a commercial airliner with a large, colourful *Mushi-King* motif.

The *Mushi-King* phenomenon is mostly unknown in the West, but Japan's affection for beetles extends much further than this relatively recent franchise. Insect collecting is a popular hobby for Japanese children, who show a fervent interest in many forms of insect life. During the summer months, when insect activity is at its peak, some Japanese department stores reserve space for insects in their pet sections, selling various species of beetles, collecting and rearing equipment, and general entomology books.[2] For those unable to make it to the store, beetles were (at least as recently as 1999) available from selected vending machines, much to the chagrin of some animal protection groups. A spokesperson for the Citizens' Group to Preserve Nature and Protect Animals complained that treating living creatures 'in the same way as soft drinks and cigarettes' sets a terrible example for children and 'belittles the value of life', adding (as if it was not obvious) that 'beetles are not Tamagotchi.'[3]

Beetle Bar,
Brisbane, Australia.

While it is already quite clear that beetles are not Tamagotchi (a handheld virtual pet simulation game), it is difficult for many to see them as anything other than 'robotic' creatures, which in turn encourages a view of live beetles as 'toys'. The practice of collecting beetles inherently positions them between subject and object, or as both: on the one hand, the beetle may be appreciated as an individual, sentient being, and as the author of its own actions; on the other, it can easily be figured as a 'mechanical' commodity to be bought and sold, killed and pinned, or dispensed from a machine like a can of soda. Toy robots are embedded in the popular culture of Japan, so it is perhaps unsurprising that beetles are readily exchanged in the Japanese marketplace. Indeed, since 2007, Japanese company Bandai has produced a line of robotic arthropod figures, called Hexbug, which includes a scarab beetle – although the 'beetle' more closely resembles a small crab.

Although the Japanese beetle craze seemed to spike during the first decade of the 2000s, even in the late 1990s a pair of rare *ookuwagata* (large stag beetles) was on sale in the Tobu department store in Tokyo for the princely sum of 5 million yen (at that time,

about £26,000).[4] In 2002 some 680,000 beetles, including more than 300,000 each of rhinoceros and stag beetles, were imported to Japan, largely from southern and Southeast Asia.[5] The market for live and pinned insects in Japan had reached such heights in 2006 that some entomologists became concerned about the international welfare of rare species, many of which commanded exorbitant prices. Two Japanese citizens were arrested in 2003 after illegally poaching 600 Lord Howe Island stag beetles (*Lamprima insularis*). In 1999 a batch of 80 live domestic and foreign stag beetles, collectively worth 8 million yen, was stolen from a Japanese store. Others have gone to even greater lengths: in Nepal, Japanese collectors have felled trees in order to access stag beetles.[6]

Apart from the *zukan* or illustrated guides to insects, translations of nineteenth-century entomology books are widely popular in Japan, too. Most successfully represented by the writings of Jean-Henri Fabre, popular Victorian and turn-of-the-century books about insects were often carefully crafted to instil a sense of compassion and wonder in readers as they introduced them to the strange and fantastic 'insect world' – a term which initially appeared in early eighteenth-century poetry before becoming established in the entomological vocabulary throughout the nineteenth century. Originally published in French, Fabre's ten-volume *Souvenirs entomologiques* (1879–1907) has been translated by numerous Japanese publishers for children and adults alike, and has inspired numerous insect films, including *Microcosmos* (1996). Indeed, part of the charm of Fabre's prose – and what makes it so exemplary of the nineteenth-century style – is its ability to address both children and adults in the same voice; despite our chronological age, we are all childlike in the face of the marvels of the insect world. In a further sign of Fabre's perhaps unlikely celebrity in contemporary Japan, in 2005 the convenience store franchise 7-Eleven released a series of collectible miniature insect figurines, including a number of beetles and a figure of Fabre himself, fixed to the bottle-tops of various soft drinks.

Beetles are among the most popular insect species. Yet the question of why insects in general, and beetles in particular, are so much more popular in Japan than elsewhere is not an easy one to answer. The Coleoptera do not feature prominently in Japanese mythology, though the god of poverty, Binbōgami, is said to have the death-watch beetle (*Xestobium rufovillosum*) as his attendant. This beetle bores into rotting wood, emitting a telltale 'clicking' sound which is traditionally thought to signal the presence of the god, or *kami*. Perhaps the insect's notorious ability to survive large-scale catastrophes appeals to the resilient spirit of Japanese society – the only society to experience, and recover from, the annihilation delivered by weapons of mass destruction. Indeed, the motifs of many manga comics speak to a widely shared feeling that post-war Japan is an authentic 'post-apocalyptic' society. Perhaps the most outstanding correlation of beetles, nature and manga is found in the work of Osamu Tezuka (1928–1989), creator of *Astro Boy* and *Kimba the White Lion*. He collected insects in the countryside as a child, and eventually incorporated the name of the ground beetle

Tortoise beetle earrings, c. 1880.

Costume design by Attilio Comelli for the Beetles in a production of *Babes in the Wood* at the Theatre Royal, Drury Lane, 1907–8.

– Osamushi – into his pen name. *Astro Boy*, *Kimba* and other highly successful animated television series were produced by Tezuka's company, Mushi Production ('Bug Production'), now located in Tokyo.

Although it is often observed that as industrialization and urbanization reduce our direct interactions with nature our interest in the variety of living things becomes redirected towards human artefacts,[7] the current state of affairs – very much exhibited in Japanese attitudes towards beetles – is one of 'in between'. Moreover, the direction of interest towards human artefacts ultimately can serve to orient our interest towards nature, and vice versa. Beetles are evidently natural, yet they seem so standardized, polished and 'mass-produced' that they are in many ways aesthetically compatible with the kinds of artefacts produced by a modern consumer economy. While Japanese department stores offer equipment for the ongoing collection of real, living insects, Sony PlayStation offers a video game, *Za Kontyu Saishu* (Bug Collecting), in which players take on the role of a ten-year-old boy and, equipped with virtual nets, jars and insect sprays, must collect 300 escaped insect species on a Pacific island, returning them to the laboratory of resident entomologist Dr Takagi.[8] Part of the cultural assimilation of the beetle involves its transmutation into a sign, or a symbol, which coexists with the real, living beetle itself. In contemporary consumer culture, however, the real, living beetle may be caught in the middle: alive, yet pre-packaged and dispensed from a machine like a toy – an animal reduced to an artefact. Ultimately, perhaps, the Japanese acceptance of beetles into everyday popular culture should serve as a reminder that, while we may be born with certain antipathies towards some non-human animals (such as insects), these attitudes are profoundly shaped, nurtured and even reversed by the societies in which we live. Moreover, the beetle has often inspired reflections on human society itself, along with notions of selfhood, and conceptions of other 'worlds' that exist parallel to our own, 'human' world.

Portrayals of anthropomorphized insects first became popular in Europe during the nineteenth century, not only with the 'golden age' of children's literature, animal stories and popular natural history, but as part of a wider scientific and cultural milieu in which boundaries between human beings and other animals were being radically rearranged. In Paul de Musset's relatively unknown *Sufferings of a Click Beetle*, illustrated by the much more widely known J. J. Grandville (Jean-Ignace-Isidore Gérard), a young click beetle is told by a capricorn beetle sorcerer that he will endure suffering all his life because he sees through social facades too clearly. A junebug introduces him to the salons, musicians, painters and females of doubtful virtue that give the insect city its character, but the click beetle prefers the down-to-earth company of ladybirds. In one of the book's illustrations, a death's-head hawkmoth (bearing the image of an exaggeratedly humanized skull on its back) paints upon a large canvas an image of tribal war between microbes within the microscopic world of a drop of water. The moth-artist is surrounded by beetle patrons as he works on the painting. We are reminded that the world of microbes that the microscope reveals within a solitary drop of water is as distant, invisible and alien to the insects as it is to us. In a reflection of the nineteenth-century popularity of representing microbes as anthropomorphized 'monsters' (a convention that persists even today), the insect-artist has *arthro*pomorphized the microbes, portraying them with a combination of insect and monstrous qualities. In conjunction with de Musset's narrative, Grandville comments on the contemporary human subjectivity within the 'human world' through reference to the subjectivity of insects within the so-called 'insect world'.

The beetle as an actor within the 'insect world' inspired Lithuanian-born Wladyslaw Starewicz, working in Russia, to produce one of the earliest stop-motion insect films, *The Cameraman's Revenge* (1912). Starewicz combined the allegorical

Scene from Wladyslaw Starewicz's *The Cameraman's Revenge* (1912).

qualities already embedded in popular representations of insects and their world with contemporary developments in cinematic, and microcinematic, spectatorship. The result is a charming and pioneering film, starring a married coleopteran couple, in which imaginative anthropomorphism, paired with a complex arrangement of multiple and conjoined perspectives, works to parody human infidelity. More subtly, the film also comments on the voyeurism of cinema, contemporaneous peep shows and human observation of insects' activities. Mr Beetle is cheating on his wife with a dragonfly dancer, while Mrs Beetle is cheating on her husband with a cricket artist. Mr Beetle offends a cricket while competing for the affection of the dragonfly at a saloon; this cricket is also a cameraman, and later secretly films Mr Beetle's forbidden tryst with the dragonfly through the keyhole of a hotel room. Mr Beetle returns home to discover the cricket artist and his wife together; he berates his wife and beats the cricket artist into submission. Later, after reconciling, the couple attend the cinema:

the film is titled *Unfaithful Husband* and, unbeknown to Mr Beetle, is directed by the cricket cameraman – who is also the projectionist. The beetle couple, along with insect audience, are presented with the 'private' moments between Mr Beetle and the dragonfly dancer. Mrs Beetle becomes hysterical, Mr Beetle attacks the cameraman/ projectionist, the projection booth erupts in flames, and Mr and Mrs Beetle end up sharing a prison cell.

The allegorical substitution of insects for human beings in *The Cameraman's Revenge* reflects a long-standing fabular tradition in which profound or universal lessons are learned from the natural behaviour of animals, or from the transposition of human traits, such as immorality, onto the animal world. It also gave Starewicz the opportunity to stage some exciting beetle battles – he had intended to use live insects to do this, but the heat from the set lights adversely affected them. But in its incorporation of the moving image as central to the narrative – it is a film about film itself being used to exact revenge – it speaks specifically to issues of spectatorship, voyeurism and truth as they appear in the emerging visual culture of the early twentieth century. This was, and remains, a visual culture that includes new ways of looking at, and representing, insects. Starewicz's insect puppets are reconstructed faithfully and to scale from their real world counter-parts and, apart from their gestures, upright postures and occasional items of clothing, closely resemble real, animated insects. In other words, the insect actors are not *anatomically* anthropomorphized. To the human observer, the world of *The Cameraman's Revenge* appears to be a private one characterized by human absence; yet this world is a curious mix of the insect (natural) and the human (cultural) with houses, cinemas, nightclubs and automobiles existing at a miniature scale and seemingly embedded in the natural world itself, almost as if the events depicted could conceivably have occurred at the bottom

of one's own garden. In its strange hybridization of the human and insect worlds, the film illustrates the ongoing entomological theme of two worlds resounding within one another, and demonstrates the power of the cinema to further reiterate this notion, visually and experientially, to audiences.

While beetles could be utilized as miniature dolls in stop-motion films, they also served as inspiration for themes of metamorphosis in early 'trick films'. In Segundo de Chomón's *Le Scarabée d'or/The Golden Beetle* (1907), audiences are presented with a conjurer who captures a giant golden beetle, which he throws into a large cauldron, upon which the insect bursts into flames. A dragonfly-winged woman then appears, hovering above the fire. The film ends when the dragonfly-woman and her two female assistants throw the conjurer himself into the cauldron, where he bursts into flames. The fantastic and 'otherworldly' qualities of insects made them suitable subjects for early cinema, much of which exploited techniques such as stop motion and time lapse; Georges Méliès' *Le Brahmane et le papillon/The Brahmin and the Butterfly* (1901) and Chomón's *Le Charmeur* (1907) are other notable examples.

Popular conceptions of beetles have, from at least the early twentieth century, become increasingly shaped by the representational conventions of motion picture film-making. As both technology and methods of film-making continue to improve, so, too, have beetles become increasingly viable subjects of visual entertainment, as further and more detailed access to their 'world' is obtained. In many ways, the filmic portrayal of beetles has continued representational conventions established by preceding media. Much of Claude Nuridsany and Marie Pérennou's *Microcosmos: le peuple de l'herbe* (1996), for example, appears as a visual homage to the writings of Jean-Henri Fabre, and at least two key scenes – the epic trials of the scarab beetle, and the hopeless loop formed by a line of misguided caterpillars all moving head-to-rear – emerge as particularly explicit examples. As with most popular insect films, the sense of wonder produced by *Microcosmos* can be seen as a product of the combined effects of the so-called 'magical' techniques of film-making – microscopic close-ups, slow motion and time lapse – in conjunction with strategic continuity editing. The employment of these techniques alters our perception of the spatial and temporal qualities of the world presented, and this sensation has traditionally been associated with states of wonder, transcendence and the arousal of the imagination. With *Microcosmos*, advanced equipment notwithstanding, shrewdly employed filmic techniques are crucial to the film's alteration of normal perceptions of scale and time, particularly as they relate to motion.

This alteration is often effected whether slow-motion techniques are employed or not, however. Early in the film, a stag beetle, appearing gigantic next to an ant scurrying by, stands tall on what appears to be a 'log'. This shot cuts to a rhinoceros beetle 'lumbering' through the undergrowth. Since the slower a creature appears to move

The rose chafer (*Euchroea auripimenta*).

156

onscreen, the larger it is usually perceived to be, the beetle seems almost Jurassic owing to its relatively large size and slow movement among the ants – it is a prehistoric giant of the insect world. When slow-motion footage of insects is employed, the effects of magnification are exaggerated further still. Compounded by the audience's general unfamiliarity with many of the insects portrayed (and hence an ignorance of their normal rates of motion), the actual passage of time within the insect world of *Microcosmos*, as expressed by motion, remains ambiguous. The beetle, as one of the film's many charismatic 'people of the grass', appears as a denizen of a wondrous otherworld, hidden in the deeper, often ignored recesses of nature.

As illustrated previously by Jung's psychoanalytical scarab anecdote, the beetle's actual residence in the obscure dimensions of nature corresponds with its metaphorical position in the murky alcoves of the unconscious mind – whence strange, even supernatural forces, perhaps embodied by the beetle itself, are prone to surface. Beetles (along with most insects) are often referred to generically as 'bugs' – which are actually insects of the order Hemiptera. But the term also connotes the disruption of a system, whether psychological (the mind), biological (the body) or technological (a computer), and originates with bugbear, bugaboo and bogey, meaning a ghost or a goblin. American Air Force pilots and astronauts often refer to UFOs, which occasionally 'buzz' around in areas they are not supposed to be, as 'bogeys'. In Edgar Allan Poe's 'The Gold Bug' (1843), a mysterious beetle disrupts the life of the protagonist by catalysing a search for buried treasure. The beetle, in this case, has been seen as a composite of two genuine entomological specimens, the click beetle (*Alaus oculatus*) and the gold beetle (*Callichroma splendidum*).[9]

The disruptive and transformative potential of the 'bug' is even more acutely expressed in Richard Marsh's Gothic horror novel *The Beetle*. Published just two months after Bram Stoker's *Dracula* in 1897, it vastly outsold the vampire novel for the following twelve months, but is comparatively unknown today. Here, the antagonist is 'The Beetle', a spectral, shape-shifting monster 'born of neither god nor man' that haunts *fin-de-siècle* London to exact revenge for the desecration of a sacred Egyptian tomb. As literary critics have noted, it is a novel in which the various facets of late Victorian modernity, such as science, parliamentary democracy, imperial identity and an investment in knowledge as a form of power and control, are confronted by the non-rational, the inexplicable, the archaic, *the other*.[10] 'The Beetle' quite literally bugged the entire Victorian enterprise.

However, while the beetle could serve in the late nineteenth century as an effective motif for everything London was not, it could also provide material inspiration for everything it held dear. When the famed stage actor Ellen Terry wore a green gown glistening with the iridescent wings of 1,000 beetles for her performance as Lady Macbeth in 1888, she caused quite a sensation.

Helea colussa.

159

John Singer Sargent painted her wearing it (the portrait is on display at the Tate Gallery, London), and his neighbour in Chelsea, Oscar Wilde, recalled the impact of her arrival by taxi: 'The street that on a wet and dreary morning has vouchsafed the vision of Lady Macbeth in full regalia magnificently seated in a four-wheeler can never again be as other streets: it must always be full of wonderful possibilities.'[11] The unique and infamous gown has been restored at a cost of £50,000, involving 1,300 hours of labour over many years,[12] and is currently on display at Smallhythe Place, Kent, where Ellen Terry died quietly in her bed on 21 July 1928.

A more recent and even more flamboyant sign of the beetle's enduringly ornamental appeal is found in the Flemish artist Jan Fabre's design for the ceiling of the nineteenth-century Belgian royal palace's Hall of Mirrors, the palace's chief reception room. The hall, measuring 25 m (83 ft) long and 10.7 m (35 ft) wide, was revealed to the public for one day only upon its completion, on 15 November 2002. It had taken Fabre's assistants four years to prepare the instal-lation, and four months to glue the iridescent elytra of 1.6 million jewel scarabs to the ceiling. The piece represents the first permanent artistic addition to the palace since Auguste Rodin produced some bas-reliefs for the building.[13] The thoroughly beetled ceiling had been commissioned by Queen Paola, and the materials sourced from the restaurants of Indonesia, Malaysia and Thailand, where the beetles are eaten but the elytra discarded. Arranged after a sketch by Fabre, various patterns can be discerned in the vast mosaic, includ-ing other animals and a 'P' for Paola. Hanging from the ceiling is a beetle-clad chandelier, which resembles a giant, rather unsettling insect itself.[14] Significantly, unlike oil paint, the deep and rich colour of the elytra will not fade over time, meaning that Fabre's installation will remain in its present, highly vibrant condition indefinitely.

In late 2012 the Katzen Arts Center at American University, Washington, DC, hosted artist Joan Danziger's sculpture exhibit

Jan Fabre, *Skull*, 2010, mixed media.

Inside the Underworld: Beetle Magic. Comprising 72 wire-framed models of various beetle species, which the artist coated in cut glass and other media, the exhibit transformed the building's interior into a strangely more-than-human domain. The beetles, of various shapes, sizes and colours – but all much larger than their real-life counterparts – were spread across the gallery's 15-m (50-ft) walls and ceilings, rupturing the purity of these blank surfaces with their charming yet disconcerting beauty. Drawing from formally accurate images of beetles, Danziger proceeded to enlarge and amplify their form both in the name of aesthetics and in order to communicate something of the magic and mythology these creatures have evoked since ancient times. The persistent ability of beetles to repulse, attract and fascinate us continues to inspire artists across a diversity of fields. But sometimes that inspiration surfaces in less explicit ways, creeping into our consciousness while escaping our full attention.

Perhaps the most ubiquitous evidence of the beetle's inspiration
of design in the twentieth century is the Volkswagen 'Beetle' –
beginning with the 1938 VW38 Saloon, and running through several
subsequent models since that time, it is the most manufactured
car in automobile history. Although not initially marketed as the
'Beetle' by Volkswagen, the name evidently emerged as a folk
expression in response to the vehicle's curved, cute, beetle-like
design. In the 1930s, Adolf Hitler was developing grand plans for
a unified, prosperous and mobile German people. An integral part
of these plans was the network of Autobahnen – specially designed
motorways – but also a car which was functional, efficient and
affordable for the public: the 'people's car'. In post-First World
War Germany, automobiles were an inaccessible luxury for most;
Hitler's goal was a mass-produced car priced at less than 1,000
Reichsmarks. This was considered overly ambitious by some, but
Ferdinand Porsche, who had already been working on a similar
concept at both Zündapp and NSU, took up the challenge. With

the endorsement of Hitler, Porsche produced the KdF-Wagen, named after the state-controlled labour organization Kraft durch Freude (Strength through Joy), part of the Deutsche Arbeitsfront (German Labour Front), or DAF. A programme was launched for workers to buy special stamps, which, once accrued, could be exchanged for a new car, including insurance and delivery charges. The outbreak of the Second World War interrupted this scheme, however, and delayed production of the 'Beetle' until after the war.

Poster encouraging the people of Germany to save five marks a week to buy a Volkswagen Beetle, 1936.

Porsche has widely been credited with the design of the beetle, yet it is clear that he did not develop it in a vacuum. The 'Beetle' bears a strong resemblance to earlier prototypes and models, such as the Tatra v570 and 77, produced in the Czech Republic in the early 1930s. Indeed, after the war, Hans Ledwinka of the Tatra company was awarded 3 million marks by a German court for his role in the design of the Volkswagen Beetle. Hitler had seen the Tatra 77 at the 1934 Berlin auto show, as had the engineer and automobile journalist Josef Ganz. Ganz had been sketching beetle-shaped 'people's cars' as early as 1923 and, three years before Hitler shared his ideas for a Volkswagen with Porsche, had designed and built the 'Maikäfer', or May Bug. The Maikäfer was the first model explicitly named after a beetle, and the clearest indication that the aesthetic

A vintage model 'toy' 1940 Volkswagen Beetle by Georg Fischer, from the Museum of Work in Hamburg.

Depiction of a beetle on public housing, Trazerberggasse 66–68, Hietzing, Vienna.

principles behind a number of prototypes and models produced by various designers and manufacturers were indeed inspired by the comforting curves of the coleopterans.

Paul Schilperoord has recently argued that Ganz, who happened to be Jewish, was 'written out' of German automobile history by the Nazis – imprisoned by the Gestapo, Ganz later fled Germany while Porsche and Hitler took up 'his' designs. In 1951 he moved to Australia to work for General Motors-Holden, and died – virtually unknown – in 1967.[15] Although it is tempting to affix the 'ultimate' design of the Beetle to a singular, visionary engineer, the Beetle was an accumulation of many ideas from many people, making it impossible to identify one person as its originator.[16] Somewhat ironically, in its defiance of a clearly identifiable origin, matched with an enduring appeal, the Volkswagen Beetle echoes the beetles themselves. So popular was the vw Beetle that it formed the basis of a successful Disney film, *The Love Bug* (1968), in which a cheeky Beetle with 'a mind of his own'– named Herbie – helps and hinders his human companions in various car races around America. Four theatrical sequels were to follow, and the films (like most Disney productions) are enjoyed across generations.

It hardly needs to be mentioned that the most successful and influential musical group of all time – The Beatles – have done

Reginald Bathurst Birch, 'The Fairy King and Queen Drawn by Ten Beetles', 1897, wash drawing.

much to keep 'beetle' well within the popular vocabulary, even if most of us don't immediately think of insects whenever we hear 'A Hard Day's Night'. Although they changed their name numerous times early in their career, eventually settling on a spelling which connotes the strong 'beat' of their music, the Fab Four briefly became The Silver Beetles in May 1960. There is a sense, though, in which the very ubiquity of The Beatles, the utter familiarity of the name, corresponds with its coleopteran counterparts. When something becomes so embedded, so pervasive, so everyday that it seems to almost transcend time, it ceases to be distinctive. Instead, it wavers back and forth, in and out of our conscious, explicit awareness, entirely conditional on our own attention. Are beetles special, or not? The answer seems to depend entirely on us.

This, I think, accounts for much of our relationship with beetles: we keep them, we kill them, we eat them, we picture them, we play with them, we sculpt them, we wear them, we watch them, we write about them, we dream them. Yet somehow they retain a powerful presence in our unconscious minds, as if they are never finally 'present' in the world, here, with us. This ephemerality, which involves more than the mere anatomical, behavioural and environmental differences between human beings and beetles, plays out across a formidable range of cultural contexts, some of which have been explored in the preceding pages. But it is this very ephemerality, I suggest, that signifies the beetle's ecological message, as it relates to the evolution and development of the human mind in nature. The beetle, unquestionably a true denizen of nature, more established, more embedded and perhaps even more significant of nature than ourselves, offers more than an invitation into the undiscovered realms of material nature itself, and more than a pathway into our cultural relationships with insects. The beetle, just as potently, provokes us to consider the undiscovered realms of our own minds – our minds as natural phenomena.

Amy Jane Tanner,
Beauty's in the Eye of the Beetle Holder, 2015.

Timeline of the Beetle

270 million years BC	230 million years BC	27,000 BC	8–18,000 BC
First Protocoleopterans appear	Earliest fossils of Coleoptera	Earliest known beetle sculpture, the burying beetle (*Nicrophorus*)	Buprestid beetle amulet is made

1828	1874	1891	1892
Charles Darwin goes to Cambridge and begins collecting beetles	Colorado beetle population explodes in the United States, threatening potato crops	Sigmund Exner publishes photograph of bell tower taken through the eye of a beetle	Boll weevil crosses the Rio Grande from Mexico into Texas, begins to decimate cotton crops throughout the South

1934	1936	1938
Lead Belly records 'Boll Weevil Blues'	Giant American toad released in Australia to combat cane beetle	First Volkswagen 'Beetle' appears

References

1 COMING TO TERMS WITH BEETLES

1　D. T. Gwynne and D.C.F. Rentz, 'Beetles on the Bottle: Male
    Buprestids Mistake Stubbies for Females (Coleoptera)', *Australian
    Journal of Entomology*, XXII (1983), p. 80.

2　Vincent H. Resh and Ring T. Cardé, eds, *Encyclopedia of Insects*,
    2nd edn (Burlington, MA, 2009), p. 184.

3　Bernhard Klausnitzer, *Beetles* (New York, 1981), p. 15.

4　Jeremy Hance, 'Beetle Bonanza: 84 New Species Prove Richness of
    Indo-Australian Islands', http://news.mongabay.com, accessed 8
    November 2011.

5　James Duncan, *Beetles* (London, 1835), p. 72.

6　Joseph V. McHugh and James K. Liebherr, 'Coleoptera', in
    Encyclopedia of Insects, ed. Vincent H. Resh and Ring T. Cardé,
    2nd edn (Burlington, MA, 2009), p. 184.

7　R. A. Crowson, *The Biology of the Coleoptera* (London, 1981), p. 1.

8　R. G. Booth, M. L. Cox and R. B. Madge, *Coleoptera* (London,
    1990), p. 1.

9　McHugh and Liebherr, 'Coleoptera', p. 186.

10　G. K. Chesterton, *The Defendant*, 2nd edn (London, 1902), p. 101.

11　George Hangay and Paul Zborowski, *A Guide to the Beetles of
    Australia* (Collingwood, VIC, 2010), p. 21.

12　Ibid., p. 24.

13　Ibid., p. 29.

14　Susan Milius, 'Beetle Fights Bass in Mouthwash Duel', *Science
    News*, CLVIII (2000), p. 229.

15 S. Milius, 'Poison Source: Toxic Birds May Get Chemical from Beetle', *Science News*, CLXVI (2004), p. 292.

16 'The Dirty Smell of Success', *New Scientist* (1 October 2011), p. 18.

17 C. G. Jung, *Jung on Synchronicity and the Paranormal*, ed. Roderick Main (London, 1997), pp. 93–4.

2 SACRED BEETLE

1 Gene Kritsky and Ron Cherry, *Insect Mythology* (San Jose, CA, 2001).

2 Charles L. Hogue, 'The Insect in Human Symbolism', *Terra*, XIII (1975), p. 3.

3 Bernhard Klausnitzer, *Beetles* (New York, 1981), p. 196.

4 Kenneth Oakley, 'Folklore of Fossils Part Two', *Antiquity*, XXXIX (1965), p. 121.

5 Yves Cambefort, 'Beetles as Religious Symbols', *Cultural Entomology Digest*, www.insects.org, accessed 17 May 2011.

6 Ibid.

7 P. Wilkinson, *Illustrated Dictionary of Mythology* (New York, 1998), quoted in Ron Cherry, 'The Functions of Insects in Mythology', *American Entomologist* (2002), p. 134.

8 Patricia Ann Lynch, *African Mythology A to Z* (New York, 2004), p. 20.

9 Cherry, 'The Functions of Insects in Mythology', p. 134.

10 Cambefort, 'Beetles as Religious Symbols'.

11 Brett C. Ratcliffe, 'Scarab Beetles in Human Culture', *Coleopterists Society Monograph*, V (2006), p. 86.

12 Klausnitzer, *Beetles*, p. 9.

13 In Frank Cowan, *Curious Facts in the History of Insects* (Philadelphia, PA, 1865), p. 30.

14 William A. Ward, 'Beetles in Stone: The Egyptian Scarab', *Biblical Archaeologist*, LVII (1994), p. 188.

15 Lucy W. Clausen, *Insect Fact and Folklore* (New York, 1954), p. 43.

16 Ibid., p. 42.

17 Cambefort, 'Beetles as Religious Symbols'.

18 Ward, 'Beetles in Stone', p. 190.

19 Ibid., p. 193.

20 Ibid., p. 199.

21 Hogue, 'The Insect in Human Symbolism', p. 3.

22 Cambefort, 'Beetles as Religious Symbols'.

23 Yves Cambefort, 'Le scarabée dans l'Égypte ancienne. Origine et signification du Symbole', *Revue de l'histoire des religions*, CCIV (1987), pp. 3–46.

24 Cambefort, 'Beetles as Religious Symbols'.

25 Jean-Henri Fabre, *The Sacred Beetle and Others*, trans. Alexander Teixeira de Mattos (London, 1918), p. 3.

26 Gerhard Scholtz, 'Scarab Beetles at the Interface of Wheel Invention in Nature and Culture?', *Contributions to Zoology*, LXXVII (2008), pp. 145–6.

27 Ibid., p. 140.

28 Cowan, *Curious Facts*, p. 17.

29 J. H. Walter, ed., *The Players' Shakespeare: Romeo and Juliet* (Oxford, 1967), p. 62.

30 Samuel Johnson, *The Works of the English Poets, from Chaucer to Cowper* (London, 1810), vol. VIII, p. 468.

31 Lillie W. Ghidiu and Gerald M. Ghidiu, 'Is your Christmas Tree Bugged? A History of Glass Insect Ornaments', *American Entomologist*, LIV (2006), pp. 241–2.

32 'Ladybugs have Northern Germany Seeing Red', *The Local*, www.thelocal.de, accessed 19 October 2011.

33 Cowan, *Curious Facts*, p. 21.

34 'Notes on Irish Folklore', *Folklore*, IV (1916), p. 419.

35 Ibid.

36 Ewald Reitter, *Beetles* (London, 1961), pp. 49–50.

37 Ibid., p. 50.

38 Edward Topsell, *The History of Four-footed Beasts and Serpents. Whereunto is now added, The Theater of Insects . . . by T. Muffet* (London, 1658), p. 1009.

39 Thea Vignau-Wilberg, *Archetypa studiaque patris Georgii Hoefnagelii 1592: Natur, Dichtung und Wissenschaft in der Kunst um 160* (Munich, 1994), pp. 40–41.

40 Ibid., p. 39.

41 Janice Neri, *The Insect and the Image: Visualizing Nature in Early Modern Europe, 1500–1700* (Minneapolis, MN, 2011), p. 6.

42 R. A. Crowson, *The Biology of the Coleoptera* (London, 1981), p. 1.

43 Vignau-Wilberg, *Archetypa*, p. 39.

44 Ibid., p. 41.

45 Ibid., p. 65.

46 Charles L. Hogue, 'Cultural Entomology', www.insects.org, accessed 1 November 2011.

47 Eric Jorink, 'Between Emblematics and the "Argument from Design": The Representation of Insects in the Dutch Republic', in *Early Modern Zoology: The Construction of Animals in Science, Literature and the Visual Arts*, ed. Karl A. E. Enenkel and Paul J. Smith (Leiden and Boston, 2007), p. 147.

3 SCIENTIFIC BEETLE

1 Dru Drury, *Illustrations of Natural History* (London, 1770), pp. vii–viii.

2 Pliny, *Natural History*, trans. H. Rackham (Cambridge, 1967), vol. III, p. 493.

3 Ibid.

4 John Scarborough, 'Some Beetles in Pliny's "Natural History"', *Coleopterists Bulletin*, XXXI (1977), p. 294.

5 Deborah Harkness, 'Elizabethan London's Naturalists and the Work of John White', *European Visions, American Voices*, CLXXII (2009), p. 47.

6 Janice Neri, *The Insect and the Image: Visualizing Nature in Early Modern Europe, 1500–1700* (Minneapolis, MN, 2011), p. 4.

7 Sachiko Kusukawa, 'The Role of Images in the Development of Renaissance Natural History', *Archives of Natural History*, XXXVIII (2011), pp. 189–213.

8 Johannes Godartius, *Of Insects, done into English, and Methodized, with the Addition of Notes* (York, 1682), pp. 106–7.

9 Ibid., p. 47.

10 Ibid.

11 Edward Topsell, *The History of Four-footed Beasts and Serpents. Whereunto is now added, The Theater of Insects . . . by T. Muffet* (London, 1658), p. 1005.

12 Ibid., p. 1012.

13 Ibid., p. 1010.

14 Jan Swammerdam, *The Book of Nature: or, The History of Insects* (London, 1758), p. 123.

15 Ibid.

16 James Petiver, *Opera, Historiam Naturalem Specantia . . .* (London, 1767), vol. I, p. 14.

17 Swammerdam, *The Book of Nature*, p. 124.

18 Ibid., p. 131.

19 Ibid.

20 Ibid., p. 132.

21 Anthony van Leeuwenhoek, 'Part of a Letter from Mr. Anthony van Leeuwenhoek, FRS Concerning the Eyes of Beetles, etc.', *Philosophical Transactions*, XX (1698), p. 169.

22 Ibid.

23 Ibid.

24 Florence F.J.M. Pieters, 'Maria Sibylla Merian, Naturalist and Artist (1647–1717): A Commemoration on the Occasion of the 350th Anniversary of her Birth', *Archives of Natural History*, XXVI (1999), p. 3.

25 Eleazar Albin, *A Natural History of English Insects* (London, 1720), Preface.

26 Ibid., n.p.

27 Drury, *Illustrations of Natural History*, p. iv.

28 Sir Hans Sloane, *A Voyage to the Islands Madera, Barbados, Nieves, S. Christophers and Jamaica, with the Natural History of the Herbs and Trees, Four-footed Beasts, Fishes, Birds, Insects, Reptiles, &c. Of the last of those ISLANDS* (London, 1725), vol. II, pp. 206–7.

29 Clifford F. Pratten, 'The Manufacture of Pins', *Journal of Economic Literature*, XVIII (1980), p. 93; E. Geoffrey Hancock, Georgina V. Brown and Brian Jowett, 'Pinned Down: The Role of Pins in the Evolution of Eighteenth Century Museum Insect Collections', *Museum History Journal*, VI (2011), p. 35.

30 Mike Fitton and Pamela Gilbert, 'Insect Collections', in *Sir Hans Sloane: Collector, Scientist, Antiquary, Founding Father of the British Museum*, ed. Arthur MacGregor (London, 1994), p. 120.

31 Hancock et al., 'Pinned Down', p. 29.

32 Petiver, *Opera*, n.s.

33 Fitton and Gilbert, 'Insect Collections', p. 120.

34 S. L. Tuxon, 'The Entomologist, J. C. Fabricius', *Annual Review of Entomology*, XII (1967), p. 6.

35 Arthur V. Evans and Charles L. Bellamy, *An Inordinate Fondness for Beetles* (New York, 1996), pp. 21–2.

36 Tuxon, 'Fabricius', p. 6.

37 John Hill, *A Decade of Curious Insects* (London, 1773), p. 4.

38 Ibid., p. 6.

39 Evans and Bellamy, *An Inordinate Fondness*, p. 22.

40 E. Geoffrey Hancock and A. Starr Douglas, 'William Hunter's Goliath beetle, *Goliathus goliatus* (Linnaeus, 1771), Re-visited', *Archives of Natural History*, XXXVI (2009), pp. 218–30.

41 C. H. Brock, 'Dru Drury's *Illustrations of Natural History* and the Type Specimen of *Goliathus goliatus* Drury', *Journal of the Society for the Bibliography of Natural History*, VIII (1977), p. 261.

42 David M. Damkaer, *The Copepodologist's Cabinet: A Biographical and Bibliographical History* (Philadelphia, PA, 2002), p. 126.

43 Richard Conniff, *The Species Seekers: Heroes, Fools, and the Mad Pursuit of Life on Earth* (New York, 2011), pp. 1–2.

44 J.G.O. Tepper, *Common Native Insects of South Australia: A Popular Guide to South Australian Entomology* (Adelaide, 1887), p. 1.

45 James Duncan, *Beetles* (London, 1835), pp. 74–5.

46 In T.R.E. Southwood, 'Entomology and Mankind: Insects over the Ages have Greatly Affected Man's Health and Food Supply and

Have Played an Important Role as Religious and Cultural Symbols', *American Scientist*, LXV (1977), p. 32.

47 In Nora Barlow, ed., *The Autobiography of Charles Darwin, 1809–1882. With the original omissions restored. Edited and with appendix and notes by his grand-daughter Nora Barlow*. (London, 1958), p. 62.

48 Ibid., p. 63.

49 Tepper, *Common Native Insects of South Australia*, Preface.

4 MANAGING BEETLES

1 A. M. MacIver, 'Ethics and the Beetle', *Analysis*, VIII (1948), p. 65.

2 Karim M. Maredia, 'Introduction and Overview', in *Integrated Pest Management in the Global Arena*, ed. K. M. Maredia, D. Dakouo and D. Mota-Sanchez (Oxon/Cambridge, 2003), p. 1.

3 C. B. Williams, 'The Field of Research in Preventative Entomology', *Annals of Applied Entomology*, XXXIV (1947), p. 1.

4 Gilbert White, *The Natural History and Antiquities of Selborne with Observations on the Various Parts of Nature and the Naturalist's Calendar*, ed. with notes by William Jardine (London, 1891), pp. 94–5.

5 Ibid., p. 94.

6 Ibid., p. 95.

7 John Curtis, *Farm Insects: Being the Natural History and Economy of the Insects Injurious to the Field Crops of Great Britain and Ireland, and Also Those Which Infest Barns and Granaries, with Suggestions for their Destruction* (Edinburgh/London, 1860), p. 1.

8 John F. Clark, 'Beetle Mania: The Colorado Beetle Scare of 1877', *History Today*, XLII (1992), p. 5.

9 Ibid.

10 Ibid., p. 6.

11 Ibid., p. 7.

12 J. Daniel Hare, 'Ecology and Management of the Colorado Potato Beetle', *Annual Review of Entomology*, XXXV (1990), p. 81.

13 'Tale of the Potato Bug', *Information Bulletin* (September, 1950), p. 80.

14 Arvarh E. Strickland, 'The Strange Affair of the Boll Weevil:
    The Pest as Liberator', *Agricultural History*, LXVIII (1994), p. 160.

15 Ibid., p. 166.

16 Ibid., p. 167.

17 John A. Lomax, 'Some Types of American Folk-song', *Journal of
    American Folk-lore*, XXVIII (1915), p. 15.

18 Ibid.

19 Russell Ames, 'Art in Negro Folksong', *Journal of American Folklore*,
    LVI (1943), pp. 244–5.

20 Ibid.

21 City of Enterprise, www.cityofenterprise.net, accessed 27
    September 2012.

22 Aphis Fact Sheet, www.aphis.usda.gov, accessed 28 September 2012.

23 L. E. Caltagirone and R. L. Doutt, 'The History of the Vedalia
    Beetle Importation to California and its Impact on the
    Development of Biological Control', *Annual Review of Entomology*,
    XXXIV (1989), pp. 3–6.

24 Joel Grossman, 'Aussie Heroine Saved Early Orange Growers:
    Australian Lady Beetle Came to the Rescue of Southland Citrus
    Crop a Century Ago', *Los Angeles Times*,
    http://articles.latimes.com, 26 March 1989.

25 Peter Griggs, 'Entomology in the Service of the State: Queensland
    Scientists and the Campaign against Cane Beetles, 1895–1950',
    Historical Records of Australian Science, XVI (2005), pp. 1–2.

26 Ibid., p. 3.

27 Ibid., p. 17.

28 Ibid.

29 Ibid.

30 Ibid.

31 Ibid.

32 Ibid.

33 Robert W. Sutherst, Robert B. Floyd and Gunter F. Maywald,
    'The Potential Geographical Distribution of the Cane Toad,
    Bufo marinus L. in Australia', *Conservation Biology*, X (1996),
    p. 294; Mark C. Urban, Ben L. Phillips, David K. Skelly and

Richard Shine, 'The Cane Toad's (*Chanus [Bufo] marinus*) Increasing Ability to Invade Australia is Revealed by a Dynamically Updated Range Model', *Proceedings of the Royal Society B*, CCLXXIV (2007), p. 1413.

34 Griggs, 'Entomology in the Service of the State', p. 23.

35 Chris Ritchie, 'Management and Challenges of the Mountain Pine Beetle Infestation in British Columbia', *Alces*, XLIV (2008), p. 127.

36 Ibid., p. 128.

37 V. Haynes, 'BC's Representational Silviculture and the Negative Affect of the Pine Beetle Animal Story', *Brock Review*, XII (2011), p. 30.

38 Ibid., pp. 25–8.

39 Edmund Russell, *War and Nature: Fighting Humans and Insects with Chemicals from World War I to Silent Spring* (New York, 2001).

40 'War Against Insects', *The Science News-letter*, LXXXVI (1 August 1964), p. 74.

41 Robert A. Haack, Franck Hérard, Jianghua Sun and Jean J. Turgeon, 'Managing Invasive Populations of Asian Longhorned Beetle and Citrus Longhorned Beetle: A Worldwide Perspective', *Annual Review of Entomology*, LV (2010), p. 526.

42 In Adam Dodd, 'The Trouble with Insect Cyborgs', *Society and Animals*, XXII (2014), p. 162.

43 Ibid., p. 166.

44 Rodger Kram, 'Inexpensive Load Carrying by Rhinoceros Beetles', *Journal of Experimental Biology*, CXCIX (1996), p. 609.

5 POPULAR BEETLE

1 Bruce Wallace, 'Look Out, Japan is in Grips of Animated Beetles', http://articles.latimes.com, 9 October 2005.

2 Akito Y. Kawahara, 'Thirty-foot Telescopic Nets, Bug-collecting Video Games, and Beetle Pets: Entomology in Modern Japan', *American Entomologist* (Fall 2007), pp. 161–2.

3 Jonathan Watts, 'Vending Machine Beetles', www.guardian.co.uk, 11 August 1999.

4 Ibid.
5 P. J. Gullan and P. S. Cranston, *The Insects: An Outline of Entomology*, 4th edn (Chichester, 2010), p. 10.
6 Robert L. Brock, 'Insect Fads in Japan and Collecting Pressure on New Zealand Insects', *The Weta*, XXXII (2006), pp. 7–15.
7 Andrew Balmford, Lizzie Clegg, Tim Coulson and Jennie Taylor, 'Why Conservationists Should Heed Pokémon', *Science*, CCXCV (2002), p. 2367.
8 Kawahara, 'Thirty-foot Telescopic Nets', p. 165.
9 J. Woodrow Hassell, Jr, 'The Problem of Realism in "The Gold Bug"', *American Literature*, XXV (1953), p. 189.
10 Julian Wolfreys, 'The Hieroglyphic Other: *The Beetle*, London and the Anxieties of Late Imperial England', in *Writing London: Inventions of the City* (Basingstoke, 2007), vol. III, available at https://dspace.lboro.ac.uk.
11 Description of 'Ellen Terry as Lady Macbeth', www.tate.org.uk, accessed 8 October 2012.
12 'The Beetle Wing Dress Has Returned to Smallhythe', www.nationaltrust.org.uk, accessed 8 October 2012.
13 Andrew Osborn, 'Insect-obsessed Artist Covers Belgian Palace Ceiling', www.guardian.co.uk, 11 November 2002.
14 Marlise Simons, 'Bits of Bugs Glow, to Delight a Queen', www.nytimes.com, 4 February 2003.
15 Paul Schilperoord, *The Extraordinary Life of Josef Ganz: The Jewish Engineer Behind Hitler's Volkswagen* (New York, 2011).
16 Phil Patton, 'In Beetle's Creation Story, a Plot Twist', www.nytimes.com, 20 January 2012.

Select Bibliography

Albin, Eleazar, *A Natural History of English Insects* (London, 1720)

Booth, R. G., M. L. Cox and R. B. Madge, *Coleoptera* (London, 1990)

Brock, Robert L., 'Insect Fads in Japan and Collecting Pressure on New Zealand insects', *The Weta*, XXXII (2006), pp. 7–15

Clark, J.F.M., *Bugs and the Victorians* (New Haven, CT, and London, 2009)

Clausen, Lucy W., *Insect Fact and Folklore* (New York, 1954)

Crowson, R. A., *The Biology of the Coleoptera* (London, 1981)

Duncan, James, *Beetles* (London, 1835)

Evans, Arthur V., and Charles L. Bellamy, *An Inordinate Fondness for Beetles* (New York, 1996)

Fabre, Jean-Henri, *The Sacred Beetle and Others*, trans. Alexander Teixeira de Mattos (London, 1918)

Godartius, Johannes, *Of Insects, done into English, and Methodized, with the Addition of Notes* (York, 1682)

Griggs, Peter, 'Entomology in the Service of the State: Queensland Scientists and the Campaign against Cane Beetles, 1895–1950', *Historical Records of Australian Science*, XVI (2005), pp. 1–29

Hangay, George, and Paul Zborowski, *A Guide to the Beetles of Australia* (Collingwood, VIC, 2010)

Haynes, V., 'BC's Representational Silviculture and the Negative Affect of the Pine Beetle Animal Story', *Brock Review*, XII (2011), pp. 21–32

Hogue, Charles L., 'The Insect in Human Symbolism', *Terra*, XIII (1975), pp. 3–9

Kawahara, Akito Y., 'Thirty-foot Telescopic Nets, Bug-collecting
    Video Games, and Beetle Pets: Entomology in Modern Japan',
    American Entomologist (Fall 2007), pp. 166–72
Klausnitzer, Bernhard, *Beetles* (New York, 1981)
Kritsky, Gene, and Ron Cherry, *Insect Mythology* (San Jose, CA, 2001)
Neri, Janice, *The Insect and the Image: Visualizing Nature in Early
    Modern Europe, 1500–1700* (Minneapolis, MN, 2011)
Pliny, *Natural History*, trans. H. Rackham (Cambridge, 1967), vol. III
Ratcliffe, Brett C., 'Scarab Beetles in Human Culture', *Coleopterists
    Society Monograph*, V (2006), pp. 85–101
Reitter, Ewald, *Beetles* (London, 1961)
Swammerdam, Jan, *The Book of Nature: or, The History of Insects*
    (London, 1758)

Associations and Websites

Beetles of the World
www.kaefer-der-welt.de

Buglife (The Invertebrate Conservation Trust)
www.buglife.org.uk

The Coleopterological Society of Japan
http://kochugakkai.sakura.ne.jp

Dr Beynon's Bug Farm
www.drbeynonsbugfarm.com

Dung Beetles Australia
www.dungbeetle.com.au

European Association of Coleopterology
www.ub.edu/aec

Roger Williams Park Zoo, Burying Beetle Repopulation Project
www.rwpzoo.org/143/american-burying-beetle-repopulation-project

Acknowledgements

I am especially grateful to Julie Harvey and all the staff affiliated with the Centre for Arts and Humanities Research at the Natural History Museum, London, for their kind accommodation and invaluable assistance.

Photo Acknowledgements

The author and publishers wish to express their thanks to the below sources of illustrative material and / or permission to reproduce it. Some locations are also given in the captions for the sake of brevity.

From Eleazar Albin, *A Natural History of English Insects . . .* (London, 1720): p. 89 (photo U.S. National Library of Medicine, Bethesda, Maryland); from Ulisse Aldrovandi, *De animalibus insectis libri septum* (Bologna, 1638): p. 76; photo Björn Appel/Agricultural Research Service: p. 111; photo Jon Avery/U.S. Fish and Wildlife Service: p. 26; Cambridge University Library: p. 106; Commonwealth Scientific and Industrial Research Organisation (CSIRO): pp. 20, 30, 131, 132; from *Current Biology*, XXV/6 (March, 2015): p. 141; from Edward Donovan, *Natural History of the Insects of China* (1798): p. 98; Egyptian Museum, Cairo: p. 46; courtesy the artist (Jan Fabre): p. 161; from Jean-Henri Fabre, *La Vie des insectes* (Paris, 1920): pp. 48, 127; Galleria degli Uffizi, Florence: p. 42; Getty Museum, California (© 2015 The J. Paul Getty Trust, all rights reserved): pp. 18, 64, 65, 66, 79, 116; from J. J. Grandville, *Les Scènes de la vie privée et publique des animaux* (Paris, 1842): pp. 58, 101; photo Brian Hansen/U.S. Fish and Wildlife Service: p. 126; photo Carol M. Highsmith: p. 123; photo Laura Hubers/U.S. Fish and Wildlife Service: p. 9; from C. G. Jablonsky, *Natursystem aller bekannten . . .* (Berlin, 1785–1806), photo Biodiversity Heritage Library/ Wikimedia Commons: p. 96; Kunsthistorischesmuseum, Vienna: p. 68; photos Library of Congress, Washington, DC: pp. 14, 118, 165; photo: Library of Congress, Washington, DC (George F. Landegger Collection of Alabama Photographs in Carol M. Highsmith's America Project in the

Carol M. Highsmith Archive): p. 123; Los Angeles County Museum of Art: pp. 45, 49 (foot); Mary Evans Picture Library: p. 147; from Maria Sibylla Merian, *Metamorphosis insectorum Surinamensium . . .* (Amsterdam, 1705): p. 88; from Jules Michelet, *The Insect* ([1858] London, 1883): pp. 59, 75, 103, 104, 148; photo National Archives and Records Administration (Still Picture Records Section, Special Media Archives Services Division), College Park, Maryland: p. 119; Natural History Museum, London (photo NHM Picture Library): p. 77; from John Ogilby, *The fables of Æsop Para-phras'd in Verse . . .* (London, 1665), photo University of Toronto Wenceslaus Hollar Digital Collection: p. 55; photo Ben Pirard: p. 43; private collection (photo Botaurus/Hampel Fine Art Auctions: p. 73; photos Lucy Ransome (University of Queensland Insect Collection): pp. 11, 15, 25, 36, 38, 39, 50, 155, 159; from August Johann Rösel von Rosenhof, *Der monatlich herausgegebenen Insecten-Belustigung*, II (Nürnberg, 1749): p. 69; from H. J. Ruprecht, *Wand-Atlas für den Unterricht in der Naturgeschichte aller drei Reiche*, III (Dresden, 1877): p. 93 (photo Wellcome Images); Science Museum, London: p. 134 (photo Wellcome Images) – this image is licensed under the Creative Commons Attribution only 4.0 license – readers are free to share – to copy, distribute and transmit the work, and to remix – to adapt the work – under the following conditions – you must attribute the work in the manner specified by the author or licensor (but not in any way that suggests that they endorse you or your use of the work) and – 'share alike' – if you alter, transform, or build upon this work, you may distribute the resulting work only under the same or similar license to this one; photo Kari-Lyn Sommers: p. 12; photo Cyndi Souza/ U.S. Fish and Wildlife Service: p. 113; from Franscesco Stelluti, *Persio tradotto in verso sciolto e dichiarato . . .* (Rome, 1630); photos U.S. Fish and Wildlife Service: pp. 10, 37; Victoria & Albert Museum, London: pp. 142, 144, 150, 151 (photos V&A Images); from Johann Eusebius Voet and Georg Wolfgang Franz Panzer, *Johann Euseb Voets Beschreibungen und Abbildungen hartschaaligter Insekten, Coleoptera Linn . . .* (Erlangen, 1793): p. 129; The Walters Art Museum, Baltimore: pp. 44, 49 (top).

Alvesgaspar, the copyright holder of the images on pp. 17, 85, Mathias Krumbholz, the copyright holder of the image on p. 19, James Steakley,

- share alike – If readers alter, transform, or build upon this image, they may distribute the resulting work only under the same or similar license to this one.

Index